POOL PLAYER'S EDGE

POOL PLAYER'S EDGE

Gerry Kanov
Shari Stauch

Human Kinetics

Library of Congress Cataloging-in-Publication Data

Kanov, Gerry, 1949-
  Pool player's edge / Gerry Kanov, Shari Stauch.
    p. cm.
  Includes index.
    ISBN 0-7360-4707-7 (soft cover)
  1. Pool (Game) I. Stauch, Shari, 1962- II. Title.
    GV891.K32   2003
  794.7'33--dc21

                                            2003008870
ISBN: 0-7360-4707-7

Acquisitions Editor: Martin Barnard; **Managing Editor:** Wendy McLaughlin; **Assistant Editor:** Kim Thoren; **Copyeditor:** Pat Connolly; **Proofreader:** Lee Alexander; **Indexer:** Betty Frizźell; **Permission Manager:** Toni Harte; **Graphic Designer:** Nancy Rasmus; **Graphic Artist:** Francine Hamerski; **Art & Photo Manager:** Dan Wendt; **Cover Designer:** Jack W. Davis; **Photographer (cover):** Dan Wendt: **Photographer (interior):** All photos © Jerry Forsyth, courtesy of *Pool & Billiard Magazine*; **Illustrator:** Gerry Kanov; **Printer:** United Graphics

Human Kinetics books are available at special discounts for bulk purchase. Special editions or book excerpts can also be created to specification. For details, contact the Special Sales Manager at Human Kinetics.

Printed in the United States of America   10 9 8 7 6 5 4 3 2 1

Human Kinetics
Web site: www.HumanKinetics.com

United States: Human Kinetics
P.O. Box 5076
Champaign, IL 61825-5076
800-747-4457
e-mail: humank@hkusa.com

Canada: Human Kinetics
475 Devonshire Road Unit 100
Windsor, ON N8Y 2L5
800-465-7301 (in Canada only)
e-mail: orders@hkcanada.com

Europe: Human Kinetics
107 Bradford Road
Stanningley
Leeds LS28 6AT, United Kingdom
+44 (0) 113 255 5665
e-mail: hk@hkeurope.com

Australia: Human Kinetics
57A Price Avenue
Lower Mitcham, South Australia 5062
08 8277 1555
e-mail: liaw@hkaustralia.com

New Zealand: Human Kinetics
Division of Sports Distributors NZ Ltd.
P.O. Box 300 226 Albany
North Shore City
Auckland
0064 9 448 1207
e-mail: blairc@hknewz.com

*To all the top players in history who have
made the game interesting.*

Contents

Preface

> "There's a perfect shot out there trying to find each and
> every one of us, and all we got to do is get ourselves out
> of its way."
> Will Smith as Bagger Vance in *The Legend of Bagger Vance*

There *is* a perfect shot, *every* time, to be had in *every* game of pool. Our challenge as pool players is to find that perfect shot, or better yet, to know our options and then get out of the way so the perfect shot can find us. *Pool Player's Edge* guides you seamlessly toward that goal.

Filled with clear, comprehensive diagrams and photographs outlining specific strategies that include hundreds of shot combinations, *Pool Player's Edge* offers new insights, new skills, and new concepts to take your game, no matter your current skill level, to the next level.

Part I offers advice on tactics and techniques used by professional players for everything from aiming to advanced shot and safety selection. Plus, we offer a troubleshooting list for the fundamentals. This list gives you the benefit of quick-fix remedies used by professional players when their own mechanics are out of sync.

In part II you'll learn the tricks to mastering the breaking and shooting patterns for the cue sport's most widely played game, 8-Ball. Part 3 is all about the pro game of 9-Ball—including racking, breaking, roll-outs, and run-outs—just as you've seen played on TV by the real professionals.

While we naturally can't show you every game and match ever played, we do use actual tried-and-true shots and safeties to describe key concepts you will encounter as you play. Every shot situation discussed and illustrated throughout *Pool Player's Edge* has occurred in actual match competition and will further your knowledge of how the pros think and react in these pressure circumstances.

Whether you are playing in leagues on the local scene, competing in regional tour events, or making your way to the professional ranks, *Pool Player's Edge* will teach you how to think like a pro so that you too can shoot your way to the next level of competition.

Acknowledgments

No book is possible without the help of many individuals. Our special thanks to Paul Harris and Rick Costello, who taught us more than we wanted to know about illustrating cue ball positions and table layouts; Harold Simonsen, *Pool & Billiard Magazine* publisher, whose insights and advice are always appreciated; Jerry Forsyth, who allowed us to view and access his substantial photo collection; and our editors, Martin Barnard and Wendy McLaughlin, who make us look good (or at least better!).

Thanks also to the many professional players who have offered their expertise, including Robert LeBlanc (advisor to the major motion picture *Pool Hall Junkies*), Ewa Mataya Laurance, Vicki Paski, and Larry Schwartz.

Becoming a Player

Pool Player's Edge is organized in the same chronological order as you might approach your pool game. In part I, "Becoming a Player," we offer a slightly more advanced approach to key concepts used by top players across the globe.

We begin with the essentials needed for a skillful pool game—the basics that all professional players return to when honing their game. After a review of the basics, including valuable troubleshooting information for problem areas you may have experienced in your game, we'll get into some of the finer points of pool, with chapters on aiming, our favorite top-shelf shots, and mapping the table (with extensive information on advanced pattern and safety play strategies).

In "Mastering the Mind Game," the last chapter in part I, we focus on the mental and social aspects of the pool player—dealing with competition, developing confidence, and playing in front of spectators. These are the kind of things you'll need to know as you become a competitive player, even in local leagues and tournaments.

Keep in mind that as you encounter information that may seem vaguely familiar, you should take the time to absorb the text and try the techniques shown in the accompanying diagrams. As most intermediate and advanced players will agree, it's the fundamental aspects of the cue sports that allow you to get an edge before you move on to specific game tactics that help you keep that edge.

The Essentials

Any pool player's edge begins with proper fundamentals. What players think of as simple mechanics will mean the difference between a win or a loss when performed incorrectly. And all professional players return right here, to the fundamentals, when troubleshooting problem areas of their game.

All players must work to achieve consistency in their game, and this starts with their body. Fundamental skills such as a proper stance, alignment, bridge, grip, and swing are necessary to play successful pool. The following sections give you a brief summary of how to correctly perform each skill and provide quick fixes for common trouble spots.

STANCE

Pros will tell you, if there's something wrong with their game, chances are it's related to the way they are standing when they shoot. A proper stance provides good balance and a foundation from which to execute shots. Here's a quick checklist to find your proper stance:

1. Stand behind a shot you are approaching at the table.
2. Line your back leg up with the line of the shot (right leg for right-handed players, left for left).
3. With the heel of your back foot planted, bend into the shot at the waist, letting your front leg arrive at a comfortable distance between the table and your back leg. Your back foot will naturally turn out so that it's more or less perpendicular to the shot, and your front foot should point toward the shot.

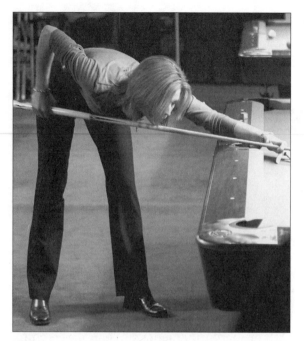

Figure 1.1 BCA Hall of Famer Loree Jon Jones stands with both legs straight as she prepares for her shot.

Depending on your height, you may have both legs straight, the back leg straight, or both legs bent (see figures 1.1 and 1.2). This is also a matter of personal preference. The important thing is that once you determine your perfect stance, you must stick with it. Too many players stand one way then change their stance mid-game, which throws off body alignment.

Of course, every rule is meant to be broken, and the rules for a perfect stance are no exception. There are times when you will find yourself, in an effort to maintain your usual stance, with your hip lodged up against the table, off balance, or forced to sit on the edge of the rail with one foot on the floor. Obviously, when you are off balance in this way, you'll find it more difficult to swing the cue tip where you intend to place it on the cue ball.

The shot shown in figure 1.3 poses one such inconvenience for the right-handed player. In a normal approach, the player's left hip would be jammed up against the short rail and

Figure 1.2 Ewa Mataya Laurance approaches her stance with the back leg straight, and the front leg bent into a comfortable position.

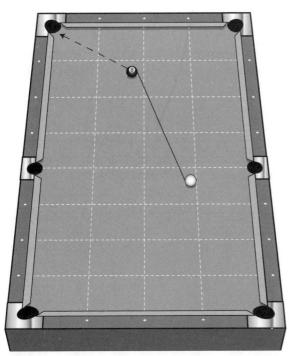

Figure 1.3 By squaring your hips up you will avoid an awkward position for this shot.

almost all of his weight would be on the left foot, and in some instances, a player might have his right leg up in the air. To avoid this awkward position, instead of angling your hips to the shot, square them up. Stand at the end of the table with your hips parallel to the rail, and then bend over into the shot. *Hint:* You may find that you must move into the shot sideways from the waist (to keep your line of aim), while keeping your hips straight.

The shot shown in figure 1.4 poses a problem for anyone who is less than seven feet tall, right or left handed. Again, the average player will

be flirting with a bruised hip and a ballet stance in an attempt to reach this shot. Square your hips to the table again, and you will find the added bonus of extending your reach. Some players, including most snooker players, square their hips on each shot. One distinct advantage to this is that their approach doesn't ever need to change.

Another situation in which we've observed top players adjusting their stance is when they approach a long, difficult shot. Hall of Famer Dallas West is one example. With a normal stance on normal shots, he would spread his feet much

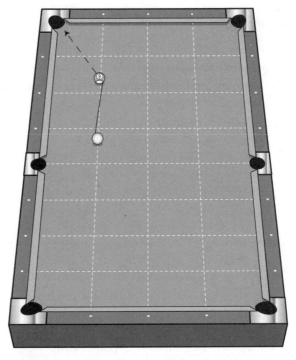

Figure 1.4 Squaring the hips allows for better balance and reach in this situation.

farther apart on long shots. This accomplishes two things. First, widening your stance gets you down and behind the shot more for an easier view of a long shot. Second, it offers the maximum feel of balance and a solid base from which to execute a tough shot. If you have a chance to see the pros live, watch for this.

Quick Fixes—Stance

If your game's not going as well as you'd like, try checking your stance. Make sure your feet are aligned, you're balanced, and that there's plenty of room for you to swing the cue. Try these troubleshooting tips to correct any inconsistencies in your stance.

- **Foot position.** If you usually hit perfect center ball on every shot with your normal stance, even a slight deviation can throw off your aim, your stroke, and your game. Try the following exercise to check your foot position.

Approach a shot and bend into the shot in your normal stance, with the tip of your cue just behind the cue ball. Now, without taking your eyes off the tip of your cue, pivot the toes of your back foot slightly forward (inside), keeping your heel planted.

Did you see the cue tip move? If you are a right-handed player, and your right toes move toward the shot, the tip of your cue stick actually moves slightly to the left. Now, try this again, this time moving your toes away from the shot (outside), again pivoting your foot with your heel planted. Try this same exercise, this time keeping your eyes down on your hips. See them move? A slight foot movement, and the whole scene changes.

Therefore, if you are a right-handed player who is consistently striking the cue ball to the right of center, your stance may require a subtle adjustment of your right foot into the shot. Periodic stance checks are prescribed for any player experiencing consistent cue ball reactions to one side or the other.

- **Balance.** If your stance is unbalanced, your body will waver as you shoot. A practice partner can help you check your balance by simply pushing you (a gentle nudge is sufficient) from either side while you are in your stance. If you lose your balance from either side, adjust your stance until you are once again sturdy and stable.

- **Room to breathe.** Make sure there's room for your cue to swing freely through your shot and that you're not too close to the table. Crowding your swinging arm or keeping your body too close to the table will adversely affect your stroke; these conditions can cause you to have a crossover in your stroke because your mind will try to compensate for bad body position. When you play in a room where tables are close together, or where table placement is too close to seating or walls, your body's natural response is crowding, so be aware of your playing conditions.

Also, stay mindful of overcorrecting. If you think you're too close to the table, don't back up so far that you're straining to reach the shot. Moderation is the key—make tiny adjustments until you arrive at your perfect stance.

ALIGNMENT

Proper alignment in pool refers to your proper head position—in line with both your body and your shot. The proper alignment allows you to easily see the shot and properly execute it. If your head is too far up or down, it will impair your ability to see the shot.

Too often, a player naturally wants to see the outcome of the shot before it has been executed. This usually results from anxiety over the situation at hand or anticipation about the outcome. It could be that you're bent too low over the shot, forcing your head up when you follow through. It could just be bad habit. Even worse, if your head moves during the shot, even slightly, your consistency will suffer. This may be the most important thing you ever learn in your pool game, so pay very close attention!

Think about how head movement affects your shot. When your head rises, your shoulder moves, your arm moves, and your eyes move off the target. You've set into motion a chain of events that will prevent your cue tip from finding its way back to the intended spot on the cue ball. In crucial situations, if you are prone to this habit, head movement will be magnified.

Typically, perfect head position will allow you to see the shot comfortably and still see the table beyond the shot in your peripheral vision. That means, while in your perfect stance, you should be bent over far enough to have a view of your cue tip and where it is approaching the cue ball. However, if you are bent too low on your shot, you'll not only strain your eyes, but you'll also need to lift your head slightly to see the shot as you follow through—a terrible (yet terribly common) mistake.

Cocking your head to one side or the other is another malady that distorts your aiming and shot-making abilities. The perfect head alignment for a player with perfect eyes would be head over cue, with the cue directly in line under the chin, and the eyes equidistant apart from the cue. But very few people have perfect eyes. Most people have a dominant eye. (To check for your dominant eye, pick up a camera and pretend like you're going to take a photo. The eye that naturally goes to the

Professional player Max Eberle aims a shot. Notice which eye is dominant as he looks at his line of attack.

viewfinder is your dominant eye.) Therefore, what looks perfectly centered over the cue to you may likely be a hair to the right or left of the cue. This is fine because your body is making its adjustment for your dominant eye.

What's not fine is trying to play with the cue to one side of your head. Yes, a few unorthodox pros get away with it, but they play more than you do! Likewise for tilting your head at an angle to the shot. And while even novice players usually know the importance of keeping their head level, this is sometimes more difficult than you'd think. When you've been playing for a long time in a session, your shoulder above your swinging arm is likely to become strained and tired. The body's way to compensate for this is to tilt the head toward the tired shoulder, protecting the muscle from further stretching and strain. The only cure is to take a break, and the best prevention is to regularly stretch and exercise the muscles of the neck and shoulder to avoid fatigue (and its subsequent compensation).

No matter how correct your head position at the outset of a shot, even the slightest movement will have a negative impact on your consistency. In fact, not keeping their head completely still while executing a shot is probably the number one reason people don't improve as quickly as they should.

Quick Fixes—Alignment

All pro players (whether they admit it or not) have had to find their perfect alignment. Fortunately, there's always a quick trick to help you with your trouble spots.

- **Height.** Figure 1.5 indicates a view from a head position that may be too low, forcing your head up through the shot. Figure 1.6 shows a view that is too high, not allowing proper sight of the cue tip to the cue ball. Figure 1.7 is the "baby bear" view—just right!

- **Centered and level.** Set up a mirror opposite your practice table, or take your cue out and get into your stance at your bathroom counter. Is your head centered over the cue? Are your eyes level and parallel to the surface of the table or counter?

You can also use a camcorder or coach to check your alignment. Another helpful technique employed by some pros, such as champion Efren Reyes, includes placing your hand on the rail of the table and checking your back and forth stroke along the rail, so that your cue travels directly on the ridge where the cloth cushion meets the table rail.

- **Head movement.** The following techniques can help you control head movement: (1) Try putting a little more weight on your front leg. With your weight distributed farther forward, it becomes more difficult to quickly raise your head. (2) Line up to the shot, take a couple of warm-up strokes, and just before pulling the trigger, close your eyes and let your natural swing take over. You won't want to lift up and peek

Figure 1.5 View is too low.

Figure 1.6 View is too high.

Figure 1.7 View is perfect.

because there's nothing to see with your eyes closed. You can't anticipate the shot. Get the feel of shooting with your head still until it becomes second nature. (3) Visualize a brick just over your head that will knock you unconscious if you jump up on a shot. Imagine that the brick will only be lifted from above your head when all the balls on the table come to rest. This will remind you to stay down and stay still until your shot is complete.

Deliver a Proper Swing

Start with a stance check. Make sure that your cue is swinging level (nearly parallel to the floor). If you're standing too tall, it's likely the back end of your cue will be too elevated. If you're too low on your shot, your back shoulder will be raised unnaturally, causing you to try to get yourself out of the way of the cue.

Next, check to make sure your arm is swinging back and forth in a perfectly forward and backward motion. Shoot a ball from one end of the table to the other with a center ball hit. The ball should come directly back to you. If you think you're aiming at center ball, but your swinging arm is tucked too close to your body, you will usually (if you're a right-handed player) put right english on the ball. Conversely, if your swinging arm is too far out, you will have the tendency to cross over the center line, putting left-hand english on the ball. Adjust your stance and your swinging arm until you can deliver a perfect straight stroke every time.

Throughout the execution of a shot, the swinging arm is the only part of your body that should be moving. Everything else stays still until completion of the shot. If you find you are twisting your body to make room for the cue to come through the shot smoothly, you need an adjustment.

As you're stroking the ball, imagine that the cue is a ball in your hand. Visualize "tossing" the cue, rather than driving it to the cue ball. Don't force a follow-through, and don't stop your swing immediately on impact. As you make contact and follow through, let the cue stick come to a natural stop. We refer to this as *letting the cue stick stop by itself*, and it's a great reminder, especially in pressure situations, to just let it happen, without forcing the movement.

BRIDGES

Your bridge hand serves as a guide that your cue will glide through or on as it heads toward a shot. It is not meant to control the cue (your swinging arm should be doing that), only to guide it. Players who begin to play the sport on their own will usually start with an open bridge as shown in figure 1.8. If learning from an instructor, a player will usually be taught a closed bridge (see figure 1.9). There has been some controversy about which method is better. A closed bridge will probably offer more control to a beginning player, but again, control should be in the back arm. As pro player Vicki Paski says, "When you use a closed bridge, you might think you don't have to worry about steering the ball. But in fact, with an open bridge, you can see problems in your stroke before they become horrendous habits." An open bridge can guide the cue while still allowing the control in the back arm. However, on shots requiring a firm hit (power shots), most pros still prefer a closed bridge so they can offer a bit more guidance up front. A closed bridge may also be preferred in tight quarters, that is, shots where the cue ball and object ball are close together.

Figure 1.8 Hall of Famer Efren Reyes demonstrates the use of an open bridge.

Figure 1.9 In this shot, Efren is using a closed bridge, offering him more control on the shot.

Another concern players have is lining up correctly, and a closed bridge can both impair your view of the shot at hand and be even more devastating if your hand is placed incorrectly on the table. We've seen one excellent problem solver in this area from pro player and instructor, Mark Wilson. Mark will line up his shot with an open bridge, then proceed to wrap his index finger around the cue for a closed bridge. We like this method because it allows you to aim and sight the shot, get your bridge hand properly placed on the table, and still result in the maximum guidance for your cue.

Several variations to these two most common bridges allow you to bridge over impeding balls (figure 1.10), bridge off a rail (figure 1.11), or bridge alongside the rail (figure 1.12). Try each of the bridges illustrated, and try to maintain a level stroke while using each one. Avoid, whenever possible, raising the butt end of the cue stick. If you must elevate (when shooting over a ball for instance), keep your cue tip as close to the center of the cue ball as possible, and execute with a short, smooth stroke.

Figure 1.10 Pro player Jimmy Wetch is forced to bridge over an impeding ball to make this shot.

Figure 1.11 Professional player Francisco Bustamante shoots off the rail with a closed bridge.

Figure 1.12 2002 U.S. Open champion Helena Thornfeldt demonstrates a flat bridge alongside the table rail.

Bridge Length

The length of your bridge refers to the distance between your bridge hand and the cue ball, typically from 8 to 10 inches. For shorter shots, your bridge will move up closer to the cue ball. For long shots (those you must stretch to reach), the length of your bridge will be greater.

Here's the most important thing you need to remember: If you shorten or lengthen your bridge, you must adjust your grip hand the same distance. In other words, if you're shooting a short "nip" shot, and your bridge is 3 inches from the cue ball when it's normally 8 inches, the difference (5 inches) is the amount your grip hand will need to move forward. Remembering this simple rule will prevent you from losing balance in your cue, which can result in an awkward stroke.

The Bridge Arm

Seldom discussed is the arm above the bridge. Some people prefer to hold their arm straight, and this has been tradition, but more and more top players have gone to bending the bridge arm. This may not look or feel as fluid to you at first, but give it a try. The bent bridge arm (shown in figure 1.13) will actually allow you to be closer to each shot without changing your natural stance or stroke. It is also more comfortable than locking and stretching the arm during long hours of shooting, and it will reduce shoulder stress.

Figure 1.13 Karen Corr's arm is not in a straight line from shoulder to wrist but is bent to allow a closer view of the shot.

The Mechanical Bridge

The mechanical bridge—more often referred to as simply the bridge—is used when a shot is in an awkward position or simply too far away. The bridge is a valuable asset if you know how to properly use it, and like any other part of your game, this requires practice.

Figure 1.14 shows proper use of the mechanical bridge to reach a long shot. Note the stroking arm position. The arm is parallel to the table, enabling the

Figure 1.14 World champion Allison Fisher demonstrates excellent technique with the mechanical bridge.

cue to be driven away from the chest as the shot is executed. When practicing with the mechanical bridge, experiment with distances from the end of the bridge to the cue ball. Find the distance between the mechanical bridge and the cue ball that will give you the greatest amount of accuracy. Hint: It's likely to be at least an inch or two closer than your normal hand bridge.

Quick Fixes—Bridge

Trouble spots with the bridge are usually limited to a few common mistakes.

Figure 1.15 2001 World champion Mika Immonen shows the use of a finger bridge.

- **Unbalanced bridge.** The edge of the palm of your hand, the pad below your thumb, and your fingers offer a triangle of stability for your bridge hand. Lifting any of these off the table will throw the bridge hand off balance, encouraging you to steer the front end of your cue stick. You may see some players, such as 2001 world champion Mika Immonen, shown in figure 1.15, shooting with a raised bridge, using the last three fingers as the stabilizing triangle. This is known as the finger bridge. The advantage is freedom of movement in your cue, much like an open bridge. It also allows for those tiny, subconscious adjustments to be made. Unless you are an accomplished player, the advantages of balancing your bridge on just three fingers are hardly worth the loss of control.

- **Bridging off the rail.** The biggest problem players have bridging to a shot on or very near the cushion is elevating the back end of the cue stick too much. This results in a downward hit on the cue ball, causing it to swerve, or massé, if it is not hit dead center on the cue ball's horizontal axis. When hitting down on the cue ball, players often fail to follow through, and this causes plenty of short-stroking maladies.

Overcorrecting, where the player drops the back end of the cue and hits the cue ball too high, can also be a problem leading to miscues and loss of accuracy. Keep the cue as level as possible, while keeping the cue tip as close to the center of the cue ball as possible. Obviously, on shots where the cue ball is frozen, or very near the cushion, you must err on the side of elevation—shooting slightly down on the cue ball is better than miscueing by hitting it too far above center. If you must elevate the cue, do so without moving it to the right or left when you raise it. Your natural body response will be to draw it in when you lift it, taking the stress off of the muscles used. If the cue's position deviates in any way while being elevated, this will result in a crossover swing, which will put unwanted spin on the cue ball.

- **Mechanical bridge.** The quickest fix for your mechanical bridging skills can be accomplished with a bit of practice and the knowledge that any shot using a bridge must still be stroked. The tendency, because you are pushing the cue away from your chest, is to poke this shot, rather than stroking it. Keeping your wrist loose is a good way to ensure a proper stroke.

GRIP

Before you get a grip on your cue, take a moment to look at your arm. Stretch your arm out in front of you, palm up, and notice how the middle two of your four fingers run in a line, through your palm, and up the center of your forearm. These are the optimal fingers in your grip hand, directing the center of power down through your arm and into your grip.

Now, grab your cue, using just these two fingers and your thumb to circle the cue. Then, let the index and little fingers circle the cue without using either of these fingers to balance your grip. Hal Mix, an instructor to several top pros, including Hall of Famer Nick Varner, advocated keeping your little finger completely off the cue, leaving it to hang daintily as if off a teacup. Keeping control of the cue with just the two middle fingers and your thumb automatically encourages a loose, comfortable hold on the cue. Filipino pro and 2001 World Pool Masters champion Francisco Bustamante, shown in figure 1.16, is one top player well known for his loose yet controlled grip.

The biggest mistake players make in their grip is taking the word "grip" literally—attempting to hang onto the cue with too firm a hold. Strangling your cue will not offer additional control, but only serve to add jerky, uncontrolled movements to your swing. The cue should rest gently enough in your hand that the hand hangs relaxed and in line with your arm, from your elbow down. Keep in mind that the grip doesn't end with the hand but extends to the wrist above it. If the grip is perfect but the wrist is twisted, this will alter your swing and follow-through.

Where to place your grip hand on the cue will depend, in large part, on the balance point of your cue and the length of your arms. The party line has been to grip the cue a few inches behind the balance point (found by balancing the cue on the flattened palm of one hand until it tilts neither left nor right). But players with longer arms (typically taller players) will not be comfortable doing this and may more comfortably grip the cue closer to the

Figure 1.16 Professional player Francisco Bustamante loosely grips his cue.

butt end (farther behind the balance point). Rather than focusing on the balance point, pay more attention to the placement of your arm—the upper arm should be approximately parallel to the floor (the lower your stance, the less parallel your upper arm will appear), and the lower arm, from the elbow down, should be hanging straight down (see figure 1.17). Your grip position will also change in relation to the position of your bridge hand, as discussed earlier in the section on bridges.

Figure 1.17 As former world champion Fong Pang Chao shoots, his lower arm hangs straight from the elbow.

Quick Fixes—Grip

Most grip problems result from mental anxiety that translates to attempting to overcontrol the cue stick with your grip hand.

- **Too loose, too tight.** Too loose and you lose control, too tight and you lose control. One method for developing a good grip is visualization. Imagine you are holding a saturated sponge in your hand, rather than the cue. Drop it, and you'll have a soggy mess to clean up; grip it too hard, and the soggy mess will be on your hands. Keep the soggy mess out of your game with a controlled, but loose, grip.

- **Changing the grip mid-shot.** Another big no-no is changing your grip pressure at any time during shot execution. This can cause lunging through the swing, steering, loss of speed control, miscues, and most important, the dreaded miss and subsequent loss of turn.

Be careful not to become fixated on the cue ball by attempting to shoot your cue tip *at* the shot instead of stroking *through* the shot. Visualize stroking right through the cue ball, and be aware of how this allows your stroking arm and your grip to stay even and relaxed.

SWING

Chances are you've seen top players play, and you've watched their level strokes. You know that your arm, from the elbow down, should swing naturally back and forth like a pendulum when you shoot. Now you're ready for a few advanced concepts.

Once you own a smooth, consistent, and straight swing, you're ready to start hitting the balls. The next challenge comes in how you prepare, hesitate (or not), and finally stroke through the cue ball.

Preparation

Even among professional players, there is no standard rhythm or timing used in swing preparation. We know world-class players, including Hall of Fame player Dallas West, world champion Mika Immonen, and national champion Vivian Villarreal, who take a few warm-up strokes and fire in their shots with no hesitation anywhere in their warm-up. Other players, such as Johnny Archer, hesitate just prior to their final swing. The cue tip addresses the ball, pauses, then pulls back and fires with no hesitation. Still other players, including world champions Allison Fisher and Karen Corr, take a few warm-up strokes, pull the cue back, then hesitate, and after this slight pause, send the cue forward through the shot. So who's right and who's wrong? They're all right, because each of these three primary methods works for those players who use it.

1. The easiest method is **hesitating in the backswing**. Take your warm-up strokes, and before delivering the final swing, draw your cue stick back, pause, and shoot. This method gives you a chance to pause, collect your focus, and zero in on the object ball before shooting. On the downside, it can also cause you to anticipate the shot, which leads to a tendency to change your grip pressure as you push, rather than swing, the cue forward. This method can also cause you to pull back too far. Instead of actually pausing at the backswing, some players continue to draw the cue back, slowly pulling their shaft right out of their bridge.

2. **Hesitating on the forward stroke** before pulling back and forth for the final swing is sometimes more difficult to master. This method offers the same chance to pause before executing, but it allows a back and forth movement in the final swing delivery. This often feels more natural and flowing to a player.

3. **No hesitation** can also be excellent. The warm-up strokes are followed by the final delivery with no break in the action, and therefore no chance to overanticipate the shot or lose focus. The downside is that achieving this consistent rhythm on a regular basis usually demands a regular playing schedule (for all but the most natural athletes). Stay away from the table for a couple of weeks, and you may find yourself naturally hesitating somewhere in your stroke.

March Back to Center

Every day your mind and body are imperceptibly different from the previous day. You may stand just slightly different, bend a bit more, or grip a little looser. Your eyes may be more or less focused. Because of these subtle changes, finding your key shot can make all the difference in your warm-up at the table. It will produce more beneficial practice sessions and more consistent match play. Some professionals refer to this warm-up as *finding center* ball since everything in pool keys off knowing where center ball is for you at any given time on the table.

Typically, a player's key shot will be a long, straight-in shot, with the object ball at least a foot away from the pocket and the cue ball straight in line toward the object ball on the other end of the table. If you can jump up and make this ball successfully from either side of the table, don't change a thing. You've come with your center ball hit at the ready. But if you're missing to one side of the pocket or the other, you'll need to make one or two adjustments to get you back on track. Check your stance, your tip placement on the cue ball, your aim, and your follow-through. Once you've got the shot down, you're ready to move on to other shots, knowing you've found your center ball for this session.

Strokes

The other quandary players experience is not knowing how many warm-up strokes they should take on every shot. Some players need several warm-up strokes (we've seen players who take more than 10!) to loosen their arm and focus in on the object ball before shooting. Others find it more natural to step into the shot, take 1 or 2 warm-up swings, and pull the trigger. Some players will take short, choppy warm-up strokes, followed by a longer swing, while others may take 3 long warm-up swings, 2 short, 3 long, and then shoot. Like determining when to hesitate, determining how many warm-up strokes to take in your game takes time to identify.

First, know what purpose your warm-up strokes serve—to warm up the arm, preparing it to deliver a smooth, level swing, and to give yourself a moment to make sure all your focus is on the object ball as you shoot. Players guilty of endless warm-up strokes are usually making decisions they should have made before they stepped into the shot. Conversely, players who take no warm-ups at all are cheating their arm out of preparing for the perfect shot every time. They may also strain their eyes, as the eyes must make the abrupt transition from a wide focus of the entire table to the narrow focus required on the object ball.

Experiment with your rhythm by throwing a rack of balls on the table and attempting to run the rack. Pay attention only to how many warm-up strokes you take on each shot. Do you take more warm-up strokes on shots you're not as confident in making? Do you one- or two-stroke shots you believe are very easy? If the answer is yes, you're in need of more practice to determine a warm-up count (part of your pre-shot routine) that works on every shot. Hint: There's no such thing as an "easy" shot. Treating every shot the same will enhance your rhythm and prevent you from underanticipating some shots, while overanticipating others.

Some would argue this, claiming that tougher shots need more time, but this is exactly the kind of thinking that leads to unforced errors. First, when presented with a tough shot, your extra time and attention should be taken *before* you step into your stance. Second, imagine yourself shooting a rack of four extremely easy shots, followed by a doozy. If you two-stroke the first four, chances are you'll rush your swing on the tough shot.

For this reason, we also recommend as few warm-up strokes as are comfortable for you. Don't assume that, for safety's sake, you need two or three more than you normally take on every shot. This may become overkill on the shots you play comfortably, and you'll lose your focus staring at the object ball longer than necessary.

Note: When learning to establish your rhythm and timing, do it in silence. Music playing in the background will influence your body's movements at the table!

Quick Fixes—Swing

Like the grip hand, problems with your swinging arm will most likely result from a desire to "micromanage" your cue stick. These fixes focus on letting go of that tendency.

- **Shooting blind.** The quickest, most surprising, and most effective way to fix most swinging problems is to spend time playing with your eyes closed. As you play, sight the shot, step into the shot, then close your eyes before you shoot. This is a great practice technique. The benefits include eliminating hit anticipation and forcing you to stay level and move nothing but your arm during the shot. You'll quickly gain confidence in your shot-making ability.

- **Losing control.** The primary reason players lose control over the cue stick as they attempt a shot is pulling back too far on the cue before their delivery. A typical backswing requires only 5 to 6 inches for most shots and perhaps 9 to 10 inches for longer power shots. To correct an errant backswing, shoot a few racks with a very short bridge so that you can't pull the cue back as far (because pulling back too far would pull the cue off your bridge hand). You'll gain quick control over your cue. You can then slowly work your way up to a longer backswing without loss of control, until you arrive in your comfort zone.

- **Crossing over.** Most players, even pros, have a bit of crossover in their stroke, which they've learned to compensate for with slight aiming and cueing adjustments. Begin every practice session and match with a few long, straight-in shots using a center ball hit. This method is called finding center ball, and it forces you to check your body to make sure you're delivering the stroke you want.

- **Crowding.** Crowding the table with your body will result in crossover problems and not having enough room for your cue to swing past your body. Step away from the table, rethink your shot plan, and then step back into it naturally.

- **Hesitation hazards.** If you find yourself exaggerating the hesitation in your stroke, forcing shots without hesitation, or hitching your swing, here's a quick fix to get your rhythm back on track. Throw all the balls out onto the table and begin shooting them directly into pockets, in any order, without the use of the cue ball. Hesitation hitches usually result from overanticipating. Shooting balls straight into pockets can help you "get your arm back."

- **Inconsistent rhythm.** Once you have determined your natural (consistent) rhythm, try humming a tune or chanting a phrase that matches it, then shoot while you hum along, matching your playing rhythm to the song in your head. Note: If you're a classical music fan, humming heavy metal won't fix your problem.

Establishing Your Routine

The pre-shot routine is your opportunity to put together all the elements of your skills and knowledge before executing your perfect shot. It's your chance to achieve consistency in your play. It's the easiest way to find a flaw in a specific area of your game, and it will offer the comfort of familiarity and the confidence of preparation as you learn new techniques and strive to improve your skills. There's no exaggerating its importance.

We've devised 10 steps that will give your pre-shot routine the direction and discipline it needs to help you execute the best shot possible.

1. **Breathe!** You're in a match and running out for the title. You just made an incredible bank shot. The crowd goes wild, everyone knowing you'll win. There's nothing left but an easy shot in the side. You jump down and shoot it straight into the rail. Or you're in a match and the score is 8-8. Your opponent misses and leaves the game ball lying near the pocket. You jump up, run to the table in excitement, knowing you cannot possibly miss this shot. You hop down into your stance, and miscue. The cue ball doesn't even come close to the ball near the pocket. You choked.

Before you laugh to yourself and claim that could never happen to you, take heed. We've seen plenty of professionals make the same mistakes. Each time the player could have avoided the mistake just by taking a deep breath between shots or a deep breath before stepping to the table. A deep breath forces you to pause, reflect, think about what's next, and perform the remainder of your pre-shot routine before careful execution of your shot. Physically, a deep breath will send needed oxygen to your muscles, allowing them to perform naturally.

2. **Step to the table.** Once you've taken a deep breath, step to the table, or if you're at the table, step toward your next shot. Often, you'll want to take a moment to circle the table to view the situation from all angles.

3. **Chalk up and scan for options.** As you scan the table, pick up a piece of chalk and chalk your cue. If you do this on every shot, you'll never have to worry about whether you've chalked up, thereby avoiding costly miscues.

4. **Decide which option you will use.** This part sounds easy, but you might be surprised to hear that even the pros sometimes slip up when it comes to making a decision before getting down on the shot. There is always a minimum of two parts to this decision: (1) how and where to pocket the ball you wish to pocket, and (2) where you want the cue ball to land. In 9-Ball, the lay of the table will determine which ball you are shooting at, but in other nonrotation games, you must also decide which ball to pocket.

Often, your choices come down to two viable options. But if you don't make that final decision before you get down to shoot the ball, chances are you'll miss, or your cue ball won't land in either place you've considered but someplace in between. You must make all these decisions before proceeding to the next step.

Chalk is Free!

None of the tricks you've seen performed on the pool table, including those incredible stroke shots, could be achieved without chalk. It's vital that you make chalking a habit so you do it automatically before every shot. You don't want to end your turn at the table with a miscue.

To effectively chalk the tip of your cue, lightly rub the chalk across the tip with a feathering motion, making sure the tip is completely covered. You don't want to screw the chalk carelessly on the tip, soiling your ferrule in the process. Avoid caking on the chalk too thick. If you do, chalk will transfer to the cue ball, creating problems; excess chalk will get on the table, your opponent, your hands, and your clothing.

The most common material used for cue tips today is leather, which suffers continual abuse from repeatedly hitting the cue ball. Chalk creates friction between the hard, curved tip of the cue stick and the hard, smooth, curved surface of the cue ball. Cue tip leather will become smoother and shinier with use, decreasing the natural friction inherent in the texture of the new leather in the process. To combat this, there are dozens of tip tappers and scuffers on the market to scuff, shape, and maintain your tip, allowing it to keep its curved shape and enough texture to retain the chalk you apply.

5. **Visualize the entire shot.** Golf legend Jack Nicklaus once called this technique "going to the movies," and he never hit a shot in practice or in competition until he could see three things in his mind's eye—the line the ball would follow to the target, the trajectory, and the spot where the ball would land. For the pool player, this translates to the path the cue ball will take to the object ball, the path the object ball will take to the pocket, and the resulting path and speed of the cue ball to its position for the next shot.

Use your powers of visualization and imagination. Visualize everything from your stroke delivery, to the object ball dropping in the pocket, to the path the cue ball will take after contact, up until the cue ball comes to rest in the perfect place for your next shot. During this step, many professionals will actually set their hand down in the spot where they want the cue ball to arrive, as if making physical contact with the table will imprint on their brain the cue ball's final destination. Try it, it works!

6. **Commit to your plan of attack.** Sometimes you're just not ready. It happens. You decide on your option, try to visualize it, and . . . nothing. If you can't see the shot, chances are you can't perform it either, so this is your opportunity to go back and rethink your plan. If it's all looking good in your mind, then you can commit, and it's nearly time to execute.

7. **Place the chalk back on the rail near your bridge hand.** You're almost ready, so declare the intention (if only to yourself) by placing the chalk firmly

back on the rail near you. It's a small, and seemingly inconsequential move, but doing so will signal your authority, confidence, and readiness to complete the shot.

8. **Step into the shot.** Step into the shot and bend over into your final stance, cue at the ready. Should you find yourself backing up into your stance, get up, step back, and then step forward into your shot. Backing off a shot isn't just a psychological defense mechanism; it can also cause you to crowd the table, resulting in a deficient stroke. Stepping into the shot keeps you on the offensive and puts you into "attack" mode at the table.

9. **Focus only on the task at hand.** All the steps preceding this should have you plenty focused on the shot, but occasionally something will distract your attention—someone running across the room in your field of vision, a hair on the cue ball, a fly trying to get in on your shot, or even second thoughts. You don't want to start over again, so you shoot anyway, then complain that you weren't ready, or that you knew that wasn't the way to go. Oh, well.

If you've watched the pros live or on TV, you've seen their focus waver, too. They're all human and subject to be distracted easily, especially when the pressure is on. But here's the difference in how the pros handle distractions: They're down on the shot, warming up, and suddenly they're up again, checking something that didn't look quite right, or waiting for a distraction to pass. When this happens, you'll also see the pro grab the chalk, step back from the shot, and step in again before continuing. They're repeating their pre-shot routine, and so should you.

10. **Shoot with confidence and authority!** Ready, aim, fire! Having performed your pre-shot routine, you can let the shot happen without forcing it, shooting with complete confidence. When the ball sinks neatly into the pocket and your cue ball comes to rest in the exact position you've envisioned, you're ready to start the process over again.

Naturally, these 10 steps won't take you nearly as long to accomplish as it's taken you to read their descriptions. But do take the time to learn and perfect each step until your pre-shot routine is a smooth little dance you can perform before each shot.

Remember, no matter how many months, years, or decades you enjoy playing pool, you'll always, at some point in your pool career, need to revisit your basic skills. Coming back to your fundamentals often allows you to discover flaws that can be easily corrected. With an eye on your fundamentals, memorize your own careful pre-shot routine, and the consistency in your pool game will increase by leaps and bounds, providing a solid foundation for building your other advanced skills.

2

Perfecting Your Aim

The number one question aspiring players ask is this: "How do you aim?" Up to now, there's been comparatively little written about aiming and aiming systems, so this chapter will help fill in the blanks for you. Aiming involves much more than just seeing the cue ball and firing it into the ball closest to the pocket. Once you pick an aiming system (we'll review a couple favorites), it's only the beginning. The real keys to aiming (the art of aiming versus the science) revolve around various "parts" of the game—short shots, long shots, thin cuts, shots using english, soft versus hard shots—and there are tips and tricks for all of them.

THE SCIENCE OF AIMING

The first thing to understand about aiming is what part of the object ball needs to be hit for it to enter the pocket. As seen in figure 2.1, the contact point on the object ball will always be the farthest part of the ball from the pocket. If you draw a line from this spot (indicated by the arrow in the figure) through the center of the pocket, you've got your optimum line of travel for the object ball.

But of course, when you get to the table, the lines aren't drawn. Finding the point of contact can seem difficult, especially on a round ball, and even tougher from a distance down the table. So, astute players and teachers created aiming systems. Keep in mind, as you learn these systems and adapt a favorite (or two) to your game, that the system—the science—works best on shots executed with medium speed and a center ball hit. The art comes in when you begin to learn the little adjustments necessary for different shots and hits.

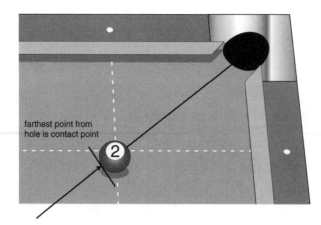

farthest point from
hole is contact point

Figure 2.1 The optimum line of travel for the object ball to the center of the pocket.

The Ghost Ball

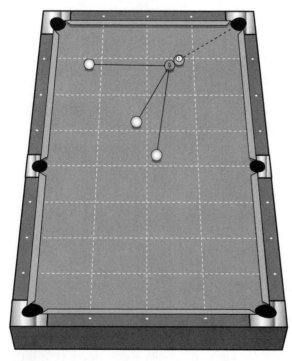

Figure 2.2 shows several shots employing the use of the ghost ball, or imaginary ball, method of aiming. To begin using this system, use an actual ball. Place the ball behind the object ball, lined up to the pocket. Burn this image into your brain, remove the ball, and shoot the cue ball to the same spot. After doing this a few times, see if you can visualize a ball behind the object ball. Shoot the cue ball to the "space" the imaginary ball occupies, and you've got the hang of it.

Figure 2.2 Aiming your cue at a "ghost ball" will move your aiming point the extra distance needed to accurately hit the pocket.

The Fraction Theory

Believe it or not, this is a system similar to that used by many top pros and much like the primary aiming system taught to snooker players in Europe. It's a great way to learn, since most beginning and intermediate players can find the "infinite number of angles" confusing. By memorizing and practicing the six basic shots in this system, you'll begin to recognize the angles, or slight variations of them, in real games. You will be able to approach a shot and think, *I recognize that, it's a half-ball hit, but a little thinner.*

This method offers an easy goal (six shots to learn) and allows you to develop confidence quickly as the shots become increasingly familiar. The basic hits include

- full ball,
- three-quarter ball,
- one-half ball,
- one-quarter ball,
- one-eighth ball, and
- very thin cut.

For examples of shots employing each of these six hits, refer to figure 2.3.

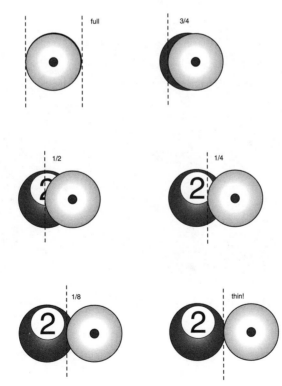

Figure 2.3 The six basic hits.

Aim Point Versus Contact Point

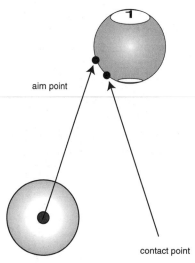

Figure 2.4 The aim point on the object ball is *not* the same as the point at which the cue ball contacts the object ball.

The contact point on the object ball (that point farthest from the pocket) is not the same point at which you will aim your cue ball (the point commonly referred to as the *aiming point*). Figure 2.4 illustrates that, because both balls are round and measure two and one-quarter inches at their widest point, the aim point will be *behind* the contact point. Again, referring to the ghost ball theory previously discussed, note that the line of aim between the cue ball and the object ball does not go all the way to the contact point, but to the space behind it.

Another way of explaining this is shown in figure 2.5. Instead of aiming the center of the cue ball at the contact point on the object ball (incorrect), aim the contact point of the cue ball (the place on the cue ball that needs to hit the object ball) at the contact point on the object ball.

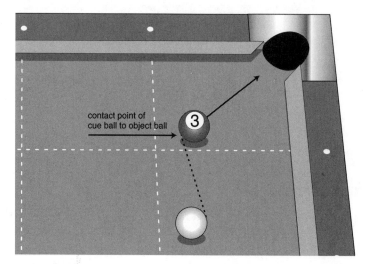

Figure 2.5 Aim the contact point of the cue ball at the contact point on the object ball.

Pocket Center

You may have heard players describing a great shot, saying they "split the wicket" or "nailed it right between the eyes." Landing that object ball square into the center of the pocket is an exhilarating feeling, especially when you know how easy it is to miss a ball by a mere fraction of an inch. Knowing where the center of the pocket is on every shot will greatly reduce these marginal errors.

Here's the secret many accomplished players still don't understand: The back of the pocket is not necessarily the center of the pocket, unless you are shooting a shot like the one illustrated in figure 2.5. But now, refer to figure 2.6 and let's rethink the corner pocket center. In shot A, a long shot down the

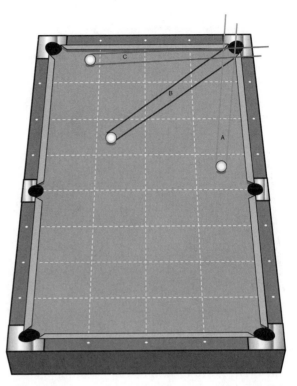

Figure 2.6 Set up each of the shots shown and get behind them to see how the center of the pocket changes as the shot moves from one side of the table to the other.

rail, aiming for the back of the pocket would result in you undercutting the ball and sending it directly into the cushion. Instead, look at the pocket opening from the ideal vantage point—behind the shot—to find that ideal pocket center. In shot B, moving to the left, the pocket opening "moves" slightly right. The right point of the cushion isn't in the way as much, and the left side won't be as forgiving. The shot "opens up" with a "bigger pocket" at which to shoot. This trend continues in shot C; the right side of the pocket opens up, and the left side closes, shifting the pocket opening again. Therefore, while the size of the pocket remains consistent and really doesn't get bigger or smaller, the opening of the pocket changes or "moves," and you must adjust your target aim to send the object ball into its center.

Finally, take a look at figure 2.7 and see what happens when you're shooting toward one of the side pockets. If the object ball is straight in from side to side, as shown in shot A, the back of the pocket is the obvious target. However, as the angle of attack becomes steeper, the opening actually gets

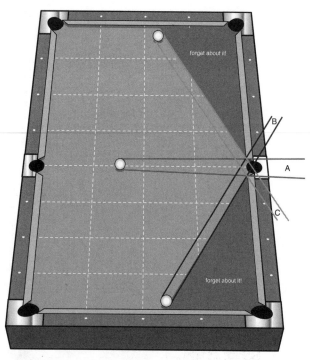

smaller. In shots B and C, the pocket center moves, just like the previously mentioned corner pockets, but it also becomes a "smaller" target because the points of the cushions can now more easily interfere with your shot. Note the shaded area in this diagram. This is the danger zone from which you shouldn't attempt a side pocket shot. The side pockets, when approached head-on, are actually bigger than the corner pockets, but as the angle of attack becomes too steep, it will be impossible to pocket a ball.

Figure 2.7 The steeper the angle of attack between object ball and side pocket (shaded area), the more difficult it will be to pocket the ball.

Pocket Speed

Along with learning the pocket center comes learning "pocket speed." Hitting the balls too hard decreases the "size" of the pocket for a number of reasons. First, with speed you lose control. Second, a shot hit softly that just catches one side of a pocket will dribble in, but a shot hit too hard will bounce off the cushions, or worse, rattle back and forth between the pocket openings and hang precariously on the edge of the pocket for your opponent! Remember, when you hit a ball hard into a rubber cushion, you compress the cushion and change the angle of rebound.

Moderation is key. Too soft and you'll "baby" the balls, which can be equally devastating. Work toward a soft to medium hit and visualize hitting the ball with confidence, but finesse. The goal is to gently drop the ball in the pocket every time, making it look easy.

THE ART OF AIMING

Before you get started, this section comes with a surgeon general of pool warning: Overdoing any of the following tricks can be hazardous to your game! And this is where the "art" of aiming comes in. A touch of this, a nip of that; these are things that work for the folks who spend a great deal of time playing. But if you haven't mastered center ball, for example, using english to aim may be a disappointing experience. Experiment with the following 12 strategies.

Thrown for a Loop

Contact throw is a fancy term for what happens to the object ball when contacted by the cue ball. Physics tells us that the balls will "cling" together for a very short time, which will result in the object ball being pushed slightly forward before taking its path to the pocket. Contact throw is present on nearly every shot. However, full hits and very thin hits have less object ball throw than a shot of 30 to 60 degrees.

There are three important things you should know about cling. First, the slower you hit the shot (assuming a center ball hit), the more "cling effect" will be placed on the object ball, making it necessary to slightly overcut your shot (as shown in figure 2.8). Remember this little rhyme: The slower you go, the more contact throw.

Second, the dirtier the balls, the more cling will be present. That's why you'll see some professionals check carefully to make sure the balls on their competition table have been cleaned. Earl Strickland, for example, insists that the balls be cleaned before every match he plays (and he is not above cleaning them himself) to ensure the least amount of cling. Third, some shots will call for very slow cue ball speeds, depending on where you need the cue ball to land. Using english can help you compensate. Outside or "running" english can help reduce cling. But most pros opt for some inside english, which will counteract the throw put on the object ball.

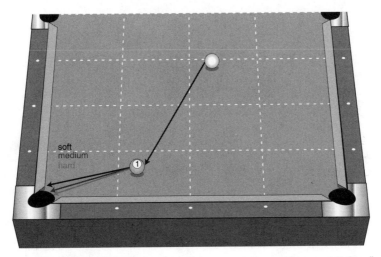

Figure 2.8 The slower the shot is hit, the more contact throw or "cling" will be present.

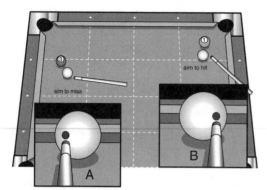

Figure 2.9 Use inside and outside english to spin balls into the pockets.

Deflect a Miss

Here's a nifty trick many pros swear by for those short, tricky shots while others never give it a thought, having long since let their muscle memory take over. You be the judge (see figure 2.9). In shot A, use outside english to spin in the object ball. Aim to miss this ball since the outside english will push the cue ball into the three ball sooner than you'd expect. But in shot B, inside english will push the cue ball away from the object ball, so you'll aim to hit this ball fuller than edge to edge contact, as the inside spin will cleanly pocket the one ball. In shots where the cue ball is farther from the object ball, this trick becomes less of a consideration because the cue ball will veer back on track due to the english being played. All tricky stuff, especially when you know that all this will depend on how much english is being used (more english equals more squirt).

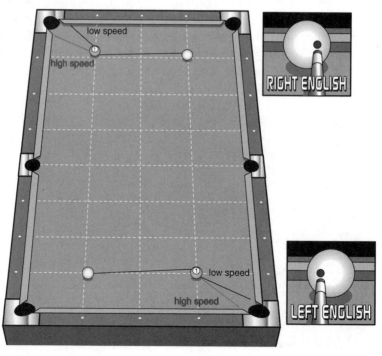

Figure 2.10 Speed variables affect aim by either requiring more or less english on the shot.

Where to aim will also depend on the speed of the shot. Shots hit at slow speeds with outside english will require less of a cut. Higher-speed shots will need to be overcut. But on shots using inside english, slow speeds require more of a cut, and higher speeds will need less. In figure 2.10, the examples show how to aim the ball slightly differently to the pocket depending on whether you are using inside or outside english at slow or fast speeds.

Stand Tall

It may sound like common sense, but you'd be surprised to find how many players learn this purely by accident. If you're having trouble sighting a shot, try standing up a little taller. Often, the distortion from looking at the shot from too low a vantage point can affect your perception of the shot. If you've had the chance to witness a match from nearby bleachers, or overhead shots on television, you know how easy everything looks from an elevated viewpoint. Apply this knowledge to your own game. If you find yourself crouching on every shot and straining your neck to see, you may want to adjust your stance to allow a better view from above.

Miss on the Pro Side

Missing on the pro side means to aim for the outside of the pocket on a shot, which increases the chances of leaving no shot for your opponent. Refer to the example in figure 2.11 and try a few of your own to get a feel for "missing safe." Remember our earlier warning? It applies threefold here. If you haven't learned to aim and pocket a ball cleanly into the pocket's center yet, take the time to do so before experimenting with this trick.

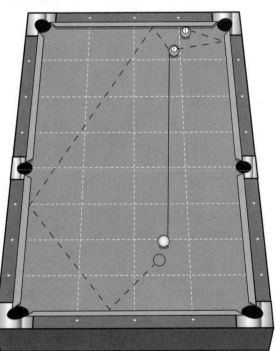

Figure 2.11 Missing on the "pro" side means aiming to miss "safe" should you miss the ball.

Aim Beyond the Ball

When aiming a shot, visualize your cue ball traveling past where you are aiming, all the way into the cushion behind it. It's easy to do on any shot, and it's an excellent visualization tool, but even better, it will help you keep your cue stick straight throughout your shot. To prove this to yourself, set up a cut shot on your table and shoot it the way you normally would, follow through, and then stop and look at where your cue tip has stopped. You might be surprised to find it has actually veered from the aiming line to point toward the pocket. That's typical, and in fact quite common, even among pros. We've watched hundreds of tapes of pros in action and found that nearly all of them end every shot with their cue pointing at their target pocket. But a rare few end up with their cue on the same line as they shot the cue ball in the first place. Most of them we spoke to, including multi-time world champion Allison Fisher, have employed this aiming visualization technique, which keeps their cue—and not so coincidentally, their shot—on the straight and narrow.

Base of the Ball

Sometimes, you lose your focus. The eyes aren't working together, you're tired, and everything just looks flat, too dark, or too bright. That's when "base of the ball" can be a real lifesaver. Sometimes, it's easier to picture the aiming line when you bring it down to the base of the ball, the spot where the object ball touches the table. It's a finite point, and it can help ground your visual comprehension of the shot. Give it a try. Use whatever aiming method you prefer, then, before shooting, look to the base of the object ball and visualize the line of aim reaching from the center of the pocket, right underneath the object ball to the other side.

The Long, Thin Cut

"Too far," "too thin," "can't see it." The top three complaints we hear on those long, thin cut shots that often seem created just to torture the pool player. A tried-and-true method has been sought by all professional players at some time in their career, and the best three pieces of advice we've learned can be combined to give you an edge over a long shot challenged opponent.

1. Think "edge to edge." When you aim the shot, visualize the edge of the cue ball heading to collide with the edge of the object ball.

2. Stick with low, center ball hits on the cue ball. Center ball keeps the cue ball on a straight path to the object ball. Low ball helps keep the cue ball hugging the cloth on its way to its destination, with the added benefit of allowing you to sight the cue ball to the object ball more clearly, without the cue in your line of vision. Many pros aim with the cue tip low on the cue ball and then raise the cue tip to the striking point only on the actual shot stroke.

3. Use as little follow-through as possible. "But," you cry indignantly, "instructors say you *have* to follow through!" Again, this is where the art comes in. With little or no follow-through, you are sending the cue ball on the straightest path possible, without any prejudice coming through from your stroking arm, especially if you're a player (like most players) with a bit of crossover in your swing.

The Long Straight-In

The opposite of the long, thin cut is the equally bewildering long, straight-in shot. Again, less follow-through can help, and center ball is a must, but the real trick here (if and *only* if the shot is truly straight in) is to not aim at all! Instead, act as if you are going to shoot the cue ball directly into the pocket. The object ball in its path will then naturally be sent in the right direction, smack into the pocket's center.

Keep It Short

What about those thin cuts down the rail? Figure 2.12 shows an example of such a shot and the way to make it easy—by pretending it's a shorter shot.

Simply pick a spot on the path of the object ball that's much closer than the actual pocket and pretend the pocket is there instead of so dreadfully far away. Keep in mind, though you're pretending the pocket is closer, you'll still need the required speed to send the object ball all the way down the rail, so practice a few until you get a feel for this method. According to Hall of Famer Dallas West, who showed us this nifty trick, players tend to become easily overwhelmed by the distance of a shot, so pretending the pocket is closer keeps things in perspective. Pretty sneaky, eh?

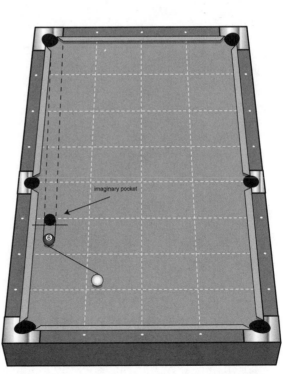

Figure 2.12 Take the intimidation out of long shots by visualizing them as much shorter and easier.

Frozen Treats!

Here are three really fun frozen ball shots that will amaze your friends and confound your opponents.

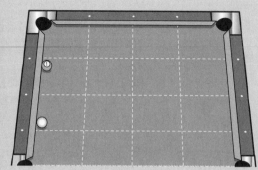

Figure 2.13a

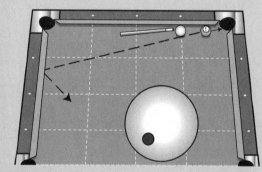

Figure 2.13b

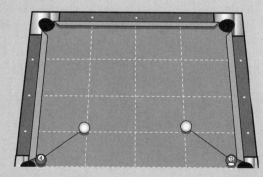

Figure 2.13c

Figure 2.13a shows the one ball and cue ball both frozen to the long rail. You cannot make this shot with a center ball hit; it requires the use of inside english, as illustrated.

Figure 2.13b also shows two balls frozen to the cushion. The one ball is roughly three inches from the pocket. In this case, you should aim to shoot the cue ball to hit the inside half of the one ball, using low left english. This shot also illustrates two concepts we've already mentioned—deflection of the cue ball and the resiliency of the rubber cushion. It'll look strange, but you should trust it and enjoy the result!

The shots in figure 2.13c require some experimentation to get them right and may depend on the equipment you use. Place the object ball frozen to the cushion adjacent to the side pocket. To begin with, the ball should stick out just a one-quarter ball past the point of the cushion, as shown. Shoot this shot hard, and the force will actually bend the cushion rubber, forcing the object ball into the pocket. Try moving the ball farther over onto the cushion. We've been able to make this work with up to half of the object ball resting against the cushion, but again, this is dependent on the pocket cut and the age of the cloth and rubber.

Frozen Cue Ball

Another long shot snafu that sneaks up on unsuspecting cueists is when the cue ball is frozen, or nearly frozen, to the cushion. It's not that the shot is tough, but the mental pressure seems to force many players to shoot hard and fast, as if escaping their jailed spot on the rail. Instead, shorten up your bridge hand (move it closer to the cue ball), employ a shorter swing, and execute the shot with soft to medium speed. This will increase your control over the shot.

The Ultimate Spot Shot Secret

Shooting a spot shot (see figure 2.14) is a lost art in today's pool games. Most games favor "all balls stay down" rules, and even 9-Ball has changed from the old "two foul" format to "one foul," sadly taking the spot shot out of the game. Yet the spot shot does still come up, depending on what game you're playing and what rule set you're using.

We went to Harold Simonsen, publisher of *Pool & Billiard Magazine* and former national spot shot champion, for his "spot shot secret," and it is presented here for the first time in print. Place the cue

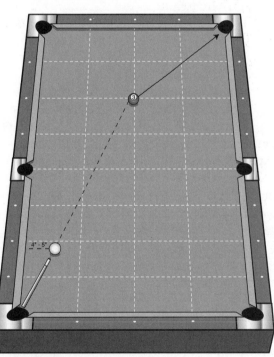

Figure 2.14 Aiming the perfect spot shot.

ball about five inches in from the long rail, just behind the head string, and place the object ball on the spot (as shown in figure 2.14). Use a center ball hit with just a touch of follow or topspin (so the cue ball will roll, not slide, toward its target). Then, simply aim the center of the cue tip to the left edge of the three ball, as shown.

For Experts Only

Our 12th "secret" is possibly the easiest to explain and the toughest to understand. Once you get a feel for aiming and pocketing balls, you'll begin to see more and more shots automatically. And you'll know, based on how you're hitting the cue ball (high, low, left, right, or any combination of those), how to hit the shot. Play even more and you might, as most pros will tell you, not even know how you aim—you "just do it." Just doing it is the category into which our final secret falls, and if you don't get it, don't worry. Come back once in a while and give it another try.

The first step in understanding and mastering this technique is to throw out everything you know about aiming. Start with a blank slate, free of method and instruction. You only want to use what your memory of pocketing balls has taught you. Now, set up a shot (any cut shot will do) and *don't aim*. Look at the intended pocket, look at the object ball, and get down on the shot with the intention of shooting the cue ball at the object ball without thinking about where to aim.

What happened? If you shot the ball straight into the rail, you're not ready for this yet. If, however, the ball went in anyway, *even though you didn't think you were even aiming it to that pocket*, you've just discovered the elusive secret of "aiming without aiming."

Again, this is pure art and has nothing to do with science. You may think with your brain that aiming full at the object ball would produce a full-ball hit, but your body knows its intended pocket and has sent the object ball there without your brain interfering, much the way Zen archers pull their bow and expect the arrow to seek the bull's-eye. If the archer does nothing to prevent the arrow from assuming its proper position on the target, then the target will be hit. If pool players have enough experience, their body and mind will also work together to shoot successfully; they just have to trust themselves and be sensitive to when things "feel" right.

This method can be compared somewhat to shooting with your eyes closed. Again, this is the opportunity to realize that your body, thanks to the muscle memory you've been building as you learn, knows what to do. When you think you're ready, throw a full rack of balls on the table, and shoot off the rack, adding position play into the mix. As you become comfortable "aiming without aiming," you'll even find your cue ball control becomes easier, as you've now begun to focus not so much on cinching the object ball, but on simply pocketing a ball on your way to lining up for the next shot. Shoot the shot, even if you think it looks wrong. Talk about increased confidence! Master this one, and we'll soon see you on tour.

CONTROLLING THE CUE BALL

Learning to control the path of the cue ball after it pockets the object ball is the greatest challenge players face. It's what allows you to get to the next shot, perform a run, and stay at the table. And learning cue ball control is a bit like learning chess, with one piece that can make all the moves. Like chess, you can easily learn how and where the piece moves, but you'll spend a lifetime attempting to master the combinations these moves can produce.

Cue ball control begins with the center ball hit. Keying off of that center, you can achieve more forward motion with topspin (follow), reverse the motion with backspin (draw), change the direction the cue ball travels after contacting a cushion (right and left english), or any combination of high right, high left, low right, low left.

And that's just the beginning. Unlike chess, where every piece has a flat bottom and comes to rest where you place it, the cue ball is round. It rolls. That means speed control. And unlike follow, draw, or english, which may or may not be needed on a shot, controlling the speed of your cue ball after contacting the object ball is necessary on every shot you shoot.

It sounds daunting, but with a healthy amount of knowledge in your back pocket, and by simply paying attention to the cue ball as you play, you'll find that developing the consistency necessary to produce runs is possible and even probable.

Cue Ball Basics

Stand directly behind a shot, and picture the cue ball as a flat, round disk. This is referred to as the *face* of the cue ball. It measures 2 1/4 inches in diameter. Now take a look at the tip of your cue stick. The cue tip will measure around 13 millimeters, which is just over a half inch. That gives you plenty of choices as to where to contact the face of the cue ball with the cue tip.

Take a look at figure 2.15. What looks at first glance like a clock face is actually a diagram of typical hits and hit combinations. Players have long taken advantage of the clock analogy, so most hit directions are automatically accompanied with verbal advice such as, "hit this one at 6:00" or "with a touch of left follow, at about 10:00."

Note from the figure that on the vertical axis, from 12:00 to 6:00, you can achieve every hit from extreme follow (topspin), down to center ball, then dropping down all the way to extreme draw. On the horizontal axis, the variations extend from extreme left english at 9:00, back to center, and on over to extreme right english at 3:00. These are the basics.

Figure 2.15 The face of the cue ball can be compared to a clock face, with each hit represented by a different "time."

The areas in between include everything from high left english (10:00 to 11:00) to low right (4:00 to 5:00), from a touch of english to extreme spin put on the cue ball. It's a lot to learn, but if you remain diligent about paying attention to where the cue ball travels after every shot with a center ball hit (as all players should begin), you will quickly learn to observe the natural reactions of the cue ball. Knowing how follow, draw, and left and right english affect the cue ball then allows you to alter those natural paths.

Finding the Center

Remember from our early discussions on stroke and stance, that if you have a slight crossover or other unique physical habit, center ball may not be exactly where you think it is, so it will pay to find *your* center ball stroke. Here's a quick and easy exercise to find your cue ball center. Replace the cue ball with a striped object ball, and line this ball up with the stripe vertical, a foot from the short rail. Place a piece of chalk on the other short rail (opposite the ball) for an aiming point. Using the piece of chalk as your target, strike the ball at its center to travel down the table, contact the cushion, and travel back to you. Shoot this shot with slow speed, holding your form, and extending your follow-through. If everything is lined up correctly, and you use a proper smooth swing, the ball should hit the rail and bounce back with the stripe maintaining its vertical position. If, on the rebound off the rail, the ball's stripe wavers from its up and down position, you will need to slightly adjust your aim to find center ball.

This may seem tedious to a more experienced player, but if you don't begin in the center, you'll never really learn the accurate path of the cue ball for all the other shots you practice. If you still think it's boring, just remember that even pros (Efren Reyes is one we know) use this exercise when they need to make their own center ball checks. Hitting the cue ball directly in the center has more advantages than the average player realizes. First, a center ball hit offers maximum control, minimum deflection, and minimum throw. Second, it offers the most predictable outcomes. In cue ball control at the professional level, predictability equals success. Third, by practicing with center ball as much as possible, you can quickly learn the "true" or unaltered reactions of the cue ball off the object ball, and you can then have a greater understanding of how spin alters the path of the cue ball.

The Straight-In Stop Shot

Learning cue ball control should begin with the most important center ball shot, the stop shot. If you set up a simple, short, straight-in shot, and hit the cue ball in the center, the cue ball should stop on impact. Note that the cue ball doesn't replace the space where the contacted object ball was. Rather, since it stops *on contact*, it occupies the space two and one-quarter inches behind where the object ball was prior to contact.

A word about physics: As you increase the distance between the cue ball and object ball, you will need either (a) more force to stop the cue ball with a center ball hit or (b) to hit lower on the vertical axis of the cue ball. Lower cue ball position (slight draw), combined with slightly more force, is necessary to stop the cue ball on longer shots because the cue ball must slide to the object ball, ideally with no forward or backward momentum left on contact. All the remaining energy is transferred from the cue ball to the object ball. Refer to figure 2.16.

The longer the shot, the greater the force and the lower the hit needed to prevent the natural forward roll

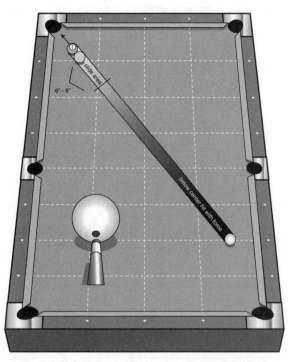

Figure 2.16 When the distance between the cue ball and object ball is great, more force or a below-center hit is required on the cue ball for a stop shot.

from taking place and causing the cue ball to drift after contact with the object ball. Gravity actually pulls the cue ball into the cloth, allowing the friction between the cue ball and the cloth to take place. The greater the forward force on the cue ball, the less gravity and friction will affect its path. Eventually, gravity and friction take over as the balls come to rest. Invest your practice time wisely by working on the stop shot, noting how much force and how low a hit are required as the distance between the cue ball and object ball increases.

Angles

So the obvious question is, what happens to the cue ball when you use a "stop shot" stroke on a shot that's not straight in? Well, obviously it's not going to stop. Again, from physics we know that hitting the ball at an angle, say a half-ball hit, will result in only half of the cue ball's energy transferring to the object ball, so the cue ball will keep traveling. But here's the cool part—with a stop shot (also referred to as a *stun shot*) on off-angle shots (not straight in), the path remains predictable.

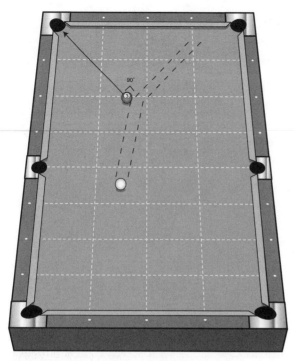

Figure 2.17 The broken lines indicate the path the cue ball takes to the object ball and the resulting tangent line path after contact.

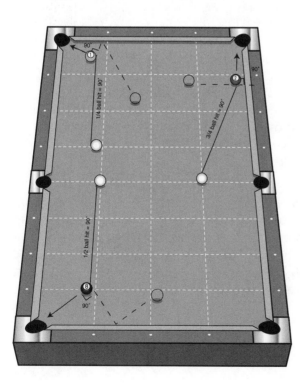

Refer to figure 2.17 to see what happens after a cue ball contacts an object ball with a stop shot hit. The direction the cue ball travels after this contact is called the *tangent line*, a line that will be (quite predictably) 90 degrees, or perpendicular, to the path the object ball takes to the pocket.

Practice each of the shots shown in figure 2.18. Use a one-quarter, one-half, and three-quarter ball hit to get the results shown. This will develop your feel for the off-angle stop shot. Next, play several racks, using the stop shot on every shot, and pay close attention to this natural reaction of the cue ball off each object ball. Note: If you're not getting the results shown, you may be hitting the cue ball too low or too high, or with too much or too little force. The cue ball must be sliding when it hits the object ball to react like a stop shot. It cannot be rolling forward or spinning backward. Adjust until you can predict the path of every shot you shoot with this hit.

Figure 2.18 Practicing each of the shots illustrated will give you a better feel for off angle stop shots.

Following Through

The follow shot is often misunderstood. If you move just a half cue tip above center ball on the cue ball's vertical axis, the cue tip will be in the follow zone. It's seldom necessary to cue any higher than a half tip's measure, and even in extreme cases that require you to send the cue ball up and back down the table, no more than a full tip above center is needed. Any more than this, and you will lose control of the shot and risk a miscue.

Here's an excellent practice technique to develop a better follow stroke. Set up a straight-in shot, and then attempt to pocket both the object ball and the cue ball. Yes, we're asking you to scratch on purpose, but just for practice. This will immediately let you know if you are executing the proper, level, above center stroke.

Play with several different straight-in shots. Once you get the feel for the smooth follow-through, try some off-angle shots. Notice how the cue ball reacts as it comes off the object ball, and how the reaction changes at different cue stick (swing) speeds. A follow stroke can be used to minimize the angle at which the cue ball travels after contact, because it will roll forward from the normal center ball tangent line, as shown in figure 2.19. The

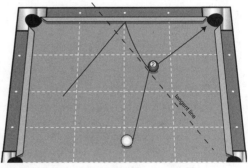

Figure 2.19 A soft, smooth follow stroke can diminish the normal tangent angle the cue ball takes after contact with the object ball.

softer and smoother the hit, the more you can diminish the natural angle the cue ball will travel after contact. This becomes useful not only in moving the cue ball around the table, but also in avoiding a scratch or other balls that you know the cue ball could encounter on its natural angle path.

Drawing the Shot

No question about it, a well-executed draw shot is the prettiest shot in pool. It looks controlled, commanding, and surprising to the casual observer, who would never expect a round ball driven forward to be able to hit another ball, pause, and spin backward. Not surprisingly, the draw shot is also a pro favorite. It offers the comfort of the cue ball hugging the table and usually enables a player to regulate the distance the cue ball will travel after contact (less distance traveled equals less chance for error).

When you practice the draw shot, you must observe a few important rules. First, your stroke must stay as level as possible, both to avoid miscues and avoid possibly damaging the cloth on the table. Second, you'll want to avoid the cue ball coming to rest too close to a cushion. It's very hard to draw the

Hidden Agendas

The cue ball does more than just roll forward with a follow stroke. To make yourself aware of these hidden agendas use a striped ball as the cue ball. Set up the shot by placing the striped ball horizontally. Then watch the actual path of this ball and observe the forward spin as the striped ball comes off the object ball. This will help you to recognize two important elements. First, you'll notice the forward spin being placed on the "cue ball." Second, you'll see that when you're cutting a ball to the left, the hit will put right-hand spin on the cue ball (and vice versa). This is called *collision-induced* sidespin or english. How much spin is transferred depends on the angle of the shot. With a thin cut on the object ball, you'll pick up very little spin from the collision of the object ball and cue ball. With a full hit, you'll also pick up very little spin. The most spin will result from an angle range of 30 to 60 degrees. Note: Collision-induced sidespin occurs on all shots, not just follow shots.

Next, experiment as you did with center ball to discover what happens with different shots, at different speeds, after contact with the cushion. You will minimize the angle with a follow stroke, but the harder you must hit the shot to reach your desired position, the longer the cue ball will remain on the tangent path before rolling forward to minimize the angle off the object ball. In other words, the harder you hit the cue ball (figure 2.20), the longer it takes for the english to "grab" the cloth because the ball is traveling with greater forward momentum, so the force of gravity has less effect.

When you shoot too high, or too hard and high, on the cue ball, it will actually leave the surface of the table, which will result in less control than the reliable friction of ball-hugging cloth.

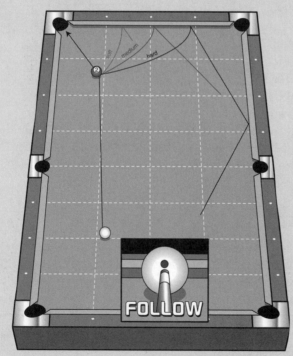

Figure 2.20 Speed on the cue ball will reduce the resistance (friction) between cloth and ball, so even with a follow stroke, the cue ball will remain on its tangent line if hit with greater force.

cue ball (and to keep your cue stick level) when it's on the rail. Third, many players assume they must pull the cue stick back quickly upon executing a draw shot. This is a false assumption—you may need to get the cue out of the way if drawing the cue ball straight back, but you still must follow through *first*. Fourth, use plenty of chalk because only the top part of your tiny, curved cue tip will be contacting the smooth, curved surface of the cue ball. Fifth, a draw stroke, unlike follow, will require you to hit the cue ball anywhere from one to two tips below center, because you will need the extra spin to reverse the normal forward energy of the cue ball. (Note: Beginners should not be trying two tips below center before developing a smooth swing.) Once you get the smooth draw stroke down, you'll find great power in that extra cue tip below center, as it can nearly double the backspin put on the cue ball. Finally, stay loose! A loose grip requires a loose wrist, which offers maximum follow-through, and thus, maximum draw.

Once you get your draw shot down, you'll be amazed by the way a simple draw shot can offer you so many cue ball control options. Not only will it allow you to bring the cue ball straight back to you, but on off-angle shots (see figure 2.21), the draw stroke will open up the angle of the shot, as the cue ball arcs back from the natural tangent path. The same physics principles apply here as in the follow shot. Specifically, the more force at contact, the farther the

cue ball will travel along the tangent line before the draw kicks in and pulls it back. Draw is also useful off the rails as shown in figure 2.22. You should practice a lot in this area because it becomes more difficult to predict the path of the cue ball into the rail after contact with the object ball, especially on shots with thinner cuts.

Using English

English, also called *sidespin*, allows you to alter the path of the cue ball by hitting it to the right or left of its center. As in the other shots you've learned, it makes sense to keep the cue stick as close to center as possible. But in the case of using left or right english, we double

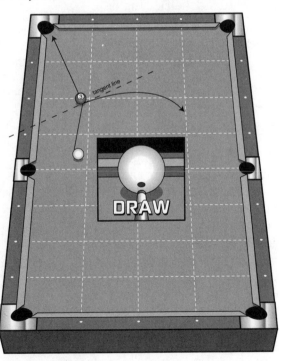

Figure 2.21 A draw stroke on this shot allows you to open up the angle of the shot, rather than the cue ball following its normal tangent line path.

the caution—lots of english is usually unnecessary, and even the pros forego using english unless it's really, really needed.

Being that it's such a dangerous commodity, the next obvious question is, why use any english at all? There are three principal reasons:

1. To change the natural angle the cue ball will take off a rail.

2. To change the natural direction the *object* ball takes (which can also be used to change the angle of the cue ball off the object ball). This is referred to as *throw*.

3. To change the speed of the cue ball off a rail.

Changing Cue Ball Angles

By using right or left english on any shot with an angle of approach (not straight in), you can alter the natural path of the cue ball and get to a more advantageous position on the table for your next shot. Refer to figure 2.23 for an initial look at how this works. Shot A represents the natural angle the cue ball will take after pocketing the two ball with a medium-speed, center ball hit. Now look at shot B. The use of right

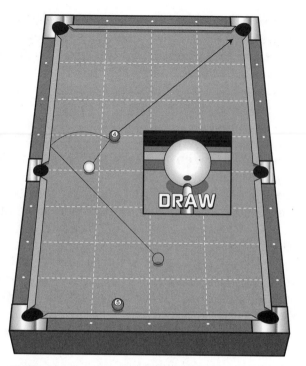

Figure 2.22 Using draw off the rail can open up even more position play options.

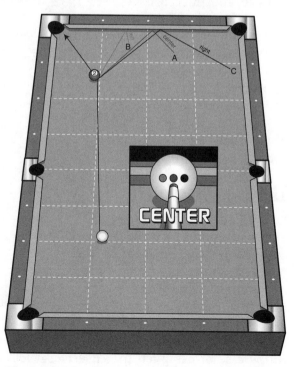

Figure 2.23 Changing angles with english.

english has diminished the angle the cue ball will take after contacting the rail. Left english in a shot cut to the left is also referred to as *inside english* or *reverse english*. Shot C, employing the use of left english, will lengthen the angle of the cue ball. Right english, in a shot cut to the left, is termed *outside english* or *running english*. Now, if the shot is cut to the right, as shown in figure 2.24, inside or reverse english (shot B) will be right english, and outside or running english will refer to left english being put on the cue ball (shot C).

Deflection, which refers to the cue ball deflecting away from the side struck by the cue tip (the cue ball will

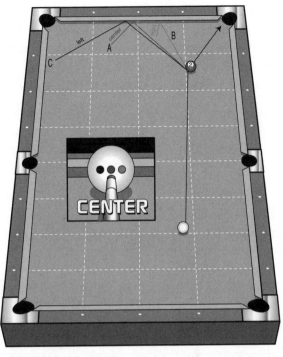

Figure 2.24 Shooting the shot to the opposite side requires opposite english to open or close the angles as shown.

deflect right when hit to the left, and left when hit to the right), also alters the path of the cue ball. The greater the english placed on the cue ball, the more deflection will result. Increased speed will also increase deflection. However, the greater the distance between the cue ball and object ball, the more time there is for the cue ball to return to its normal path.

Changing Object Ball Paths

As we already discussed in the section on aiming, contact throw is present on every shot, except for the straight-in variety. This throw can be increased with the use of english because the cue ball spins in one direction, which, like a gear, forces the object ball to spin in the opposite direction. Conversely, if you would naturally throw a ball one direction because of the angle of the shot, using the opposite english can decrease the contact throw. If you are using right english, you will put left spin on the object ball or "throw" it to the left, and vice versa. In the opposite of deflection, the softer the shot is hit, the more throw will be imparted on the object ball. It's important to understand what effect english has on the object ball as well as the cue ball.

Frankly though, the most important reason to understand terms like *deflection* and *contact throw* is to avoid the greatest pitfall of all—the dreaded cue ball control syndrome (CBCS). A common disease among players aspiring to greatness,

CBCS is caused by a keen desire to get your cue ball to the perfect location for your next shot, while sacrificing the accuracy of your current shot. Remember, it doesn't matter how good your shape is after a shot if you miss the shot!

Combined Effects of Spin

Center. Low. High. Right. Left. Once you get a feel for the basics, you'll quickly realize that these can be combined for the ultimate in cue ball control versatility. Back to the clock face, no longer are you limited to 12:00, 3:00, 6:00, and 9:00. Moving clockwise from high noon, there's high right (1:00 to 2:00), low right (4:00 to 5:00), low left (7:00 to 8:00), and high left (10:00 to 11:00). The best way to learn each of these variations is through your own careful experimentation. With the use of several different angles, cut both to the left and to the right, you can execute shots intended to arrive at virtually any position you can imagine.

CHECKING YOUR SPEED

Conjure up an image of speed control, and whether you have kids—or are a kid—chances are that image comes with a joystick and a video race car game. But in pool, speed control requires much more than fingertip dexterity. Knowledge, feel, and pinpoint accuracy in this game of inches are all required to produce the kind of speed control on the cue ball that will keep you at the table.

The most difficult thing to acquire in pool is the touch or feel when hitting the cue ball. How far will it go after contacting the object ball? How far will it rebound off the first, second, or third rail? Controlling the speed of the cue ball on any given shot will depend on several different factors.

Grip Pressure

Adjusting the pressure of your grip can change the speed the cue ball will take after contacting the tip of the cue stick. As we discussed earlier, it's always better to keep a loose grip, but as your game develops, you'll want to experiment with tightening up your grip (not strangling it, just some increased pressure) on shots where you need the cue ball to travel a shorter distance. Set up a simple off-angle shot, and shoot it center ball with a loose grip. Then shoot the same shot at the same speed of stroke, slightly increasing your grip pressure, and gauge the results. The important thing to note here is that you should *not* change the grip pressure during your swing. Decide on your grip pressure for the shot and stick to it.

Hard Swings

Controlling your shot with proper cue stick speed is required for every shot you attempt, but 99 percent of players tend to hit the cue ball way too hard.

In order to move from point A to point B, the average player thinks she must really crank up and let go with that swing. Nothing could be further from the truth. The ball is round. It will roll for a long time, even with the friction between the cloth and the ball slowing it down.

By using a soft hit, you will quickly learn a couple of pool truths. You'll notice it's much easier to pocket balls. The pocket will accept the ball more willingly, effectively making the pocket "bigger." Try shooting the ball just hard enough to make the object ball in the hole. You will see that even some mis-hits will fall. This is referred to as *pocket speed*, shooting a ball just hard enough to reach the pocket and softly plop into darkness. And by not hitting so hard, the cue ball will be easier to control.

How hard is too hard? Well, that depends on your shot. But for the purposes of this discussion, a soft hit would be shooting the cue ball lengthwise from one end of the table to the other, a medium hit would be down and back, and a hard hit would be down and back, and back again toward the other end.

If you discover you're shooting too hard on most shots, even in practice, try shortening the distance between your bridge hand and the cue ball. The greater the distance between your bridge hand and the tip of the cue stick, the farther the cue ball will travel given the same stroke. Next, remember that as you increase the velocity of your swing, you will increase the speed of the cue ball, so slow down!

Speed Laws of Physics

Physics tells us that if you hit an object ball full with the cue ball, and both balls weigh the same, the energy from the cue ball will be transferred to the object ball, and the cue ball will stop moving (as in the stop shot). Full or nearly full ball hits will require greater force or the use of follow, draw, or english if you want to move the cue ball more than a few inches after contact.

Conversely, a long thin cut will require a harder hit on the cue ball, since little energy is being transferred to the object ball. Therefore, since little energy is transferred to the object ball, it's much more difficult to control the speed of the cue ball.

What all this means is that the optimum speed control will come from setting up for shots that give you a bit of an angle to work with, but not so much as to have to turn the cue ball loose on the table.

Cushioning the Blow

The cushions bordering the table can be effectively used to control your cue ball speed. The softer the hit into the cushion, the more speed will be taken off the cue ball as it leaves the rail. The harder the hit into the cushion, the less speed will be taken off because the cushion is rubber and the cue ball will spring off it on impact. Multiple cushions provide more options, as each subsequent contact with a cushion by the cue ball removes more energy from the cue ball.

English Speaking Cue Balls

Follow and draw will obviously affect the speed of the cue ball after contact, producing a forward rolling motion, or backward drag, respectively. But left and right english can also contribute to speed control if properly used. Inside english (right spin if cutting a ball right, left if cutting a ball to the left) can be used to slow the cue ball down or "stun" it after impact with the object ball. Extreme angle shots require experience and feel to accomplish this. Outside english (also called *running english* for this very reason) will cause the cue ball to "run" or roll farther. Say you decide that you need inside english for position on a shot, but still need to send the cue ball farther than it would normally travel. Knowing that inside english slows the shot down should tell you that you'll need to hit it firmer to send the cue ball the same distance it would travel with the same cue stick speed on a center ball hit.

Elements Beyond Your Control

Just when you think you've got the hang of the whole speed control mess, you play at a club or tournament with unfamiliar conditions, and your whole game heads south. Knowing how various parts of equipment on a pool table react will allow you to quickly adjust to new conditions, just as professionals must do in every tournament they enter.

- **Cloth.** The fabric covering the slate bed and rubber cushions on a pool table, sometimes referred to as *felt* (though it's really worsted wool), produces the biggest condition variables in pool. New cloth is fast and slick. It might have even come with a slight "finish" that produces plenty of skids until the cloth is broken in. Chalk and dust haven't had a chance to work their way into the fibers, and this contributes to high speeds. And installation of new cloth requires stretching the cloth over the slate bed. Tightly stretched cloth will play faster, while older cloths will have lost some of that stretch due to continual wear and tear. Chalk and dust get between the fibers, further slowing things down. But, if the cloth is very old, it will become extremely worn and thin (even shiny in spots) and will play quite fast again because there will be less friction between the cloth and the balls.

- **Cushions.** New cushions play fast, while the rubber in older cushions begins to break down and become unstable and unpredictable. In addition, cushions, which are glued to the rails of a table, can become unglued through wear and tear, producing what's called a *dead spot* on the rail. Shooting a ball into this spot will produce a sort of "splat" rather than a natural rebound reaction.

  Finally, different textures of rubber and the profiles (height) of cushions used by different manufacturers will also produce different results. Cushions higher than normal produce different rebound results, causing the ball to come off the rail at a lesser angle.

- **Balls.** Balls once produced from ivory have been replaced by balls produced from the more elastic and better wearing phenolic resins, though cheaper brands may be manufactured from less expensive plastics (these will chip, dent, and break).

  Dirty pool balls will not roll true and have a tendency to stick together on impact. Conversely, waxed balls are equally devastating to your game, causing unwanted skids.

- **Weather.** While it's true we haven't heard of many pool games getting rained out or stopped for lightning delays, today's weather may indeed affect your pool game, simply because of humidity. You may have seen professional players interviewed on television about climate changes in the finals of an event. Often, hot TV lights will "dry out" a table. But a big crowd of people, all breathing and sweating in a small space, will quickly increase the humidity factor.

Humidity will wreak havoc on a player's game because it so greatly determines the playing conditions of the cloth, cushions, and balls, and it can change from hour to hour. Cloth absorbs the water and will play more slowly (like a dew-covered golf green). You'd also expect cushions to play slowly because they're covered by the damp cloth, but that doesn't hold true. Rubber, when wet, actually becomes more "springy." The older the cushions, the more water they'll soak up (because they break down and become more porous), making them "juicy" enough to actually spit a ball from the cushion at nearly the speed at which it arrived, and at more acute angles (think Superball!). Finally, the balls will also be affected by surface condensation, producing more friction on the cloth, and more cling between each other.

The biggest mistake you can make as a player is to obsess over conditions you can't control. This will hamper the rest of your game. Instead, make a quick analysis of what you've got to work with, then use your knowledge to play through the circumstances. And a final hint: When shooting on unfamiliar equipment, or equipment you know may suffer from any of the maladies we've described, stay as close to center ball as possible on all shots. This will greatly increase your control over the poor conditions.

No matter how long you've played pool, the variables surrounding the mysteries of aiming never cease to surprise even the most accomplished player. Hitting a curved cue tip into a round ball to pocket another round ball offers a myriad of options. Your eyes offer many more illusions and tricks at your disposal. And, the more familiar you become with your own game, the less time you'll spend "aiming" shots, as your muscle memory takes over and your mind moves onto other challenges of the game.

Top-Shelf Shots

3

All professional players have their favorite—and least favorite—top-shelf shots. These are the critical shots they become known for executing with style, or sometimes even known for missing! Some pros are known for their extraordinary jumping skills. (Six-time world champion Earl Strickland, who made the jump shot famous before players were using jump cues, is one such player.) Others are known for their skills at banking. (Hall of Famer Eddie Taylor, the "Knoxville Bear," was arguably the best banking player ever.) Flip that coin and you'll have players known for their inability to consistently produce some shots.

It stands to reason that you'll also find certain critical shots that come naturally to you, while other shots will give you fits. That's perfectly normal. However, with a working knowledge of top-shelf shots, you are guaranteed more options at the table in every game you play. Top-shelf shots include

- stop shots,
- the frozen ball,
- bank shots,
- kick shots,
- combinations,
- caroms,
- the billiard shot,
- jump shots, and
- curve shots.

Treat each of these shots with care, building each one as you would work out to build a major muscle group. As an added plus to building these skills, knowing you've got an arsenal of top-shelf shots in your bag is a fantastic confidence booster.

STOP SHOTS

Stop shots, and their stun and drag variations, offer a huge advantage to your game—predictability. These shots are more predictable because you control the cue ball to the greatest degree, with little or no movement after contact with the object ball. As you learned earlier in our discussions of center ball, a straight-in stop shot offers the greatest predictability. The cue ball will come to rest at the exact spot where it contacts the object ball.

When executed on a shot that is not straight in, a stop shot is more often referred to as a *stun shot*. The cue ball will come off at a 90-degree angle from its contact with the object ball (the tangent line) and travel as far as the energy left on the cue ball will take it. Nearly full ball hits with slight angles offer more control, while thin cuts will send the cue ball a greater distance.

A *drag shot* is used to send the cue ball a few inches beyond where it contacts the object ball, letting it "drift" into easy position for your next shot. As opposed to the stop and stun shots, where no forward momentum should be left on the cue ball as it slides into the object ball, a drag shot will leave a bit of forward roll on the cue ball upon contact.

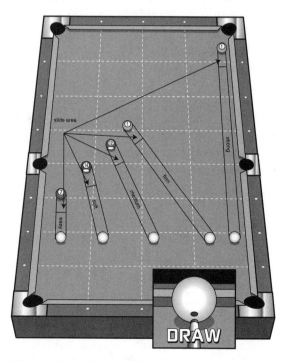

Figure 3.1 Hit the ball lower and harder as distance increases between the cue ball and object ball.

Building your skills on these shots, as in all top-shelf shots, requires some focused practice or drills. In each of the drills shown in figure 3.1 through 3.3, attempt to imitate the results shown, and pay strict attention to the reaction of your cue ball upon contact with the object ball. Note that as you proceed through the shots in each drill, you will need to increase the speed (force) of the shot or hit farther below center on the cue ball. You'll find that a combination of these works well. Next, try achieving each result without increasing the force of your hit and only varying the below center hit on the cue ball. This might take more practice, but the payoff will be more control.

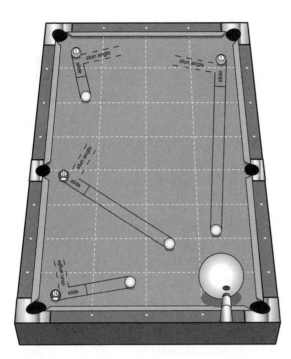

Figure 3.2 Pay strict attention to the line the cue ball travels in each of the stun shots illustrated.

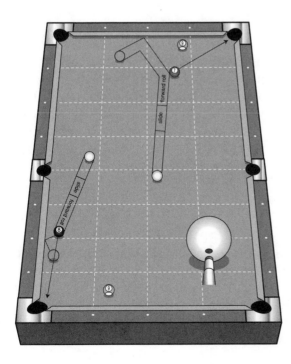

Figure 3.3 It is important to note where the cue ball hits the cushion after each shot.

THE FROZEN BALL

A frozen ball shot refers to when the object ball is frozen to (touching) a cushion. A frozen ball shot is really quite simple, but we call it a top-shelf shot because many players don't take the extra step necessary to learn the skills needed to consistently pocket this type of shot.

The secret many pros may claim to know is called *downstroking* the cue ball to pocket the frozen ball, which means beginning with a center (or above center) ball hit and aiming the cue tip farther below center on the follow-through. What those same pros don't know is that this is a bad explanation of a good idea. You're not really downstroking the ball at all—you're simply exaggerating your follow-through, and this results in a firm, full hit. This method also keeps you focused on the shot at hand, rather than fearing the shot, which can translate to poor follow-through and a miss.

Where you need your cue ball to end up after pocketing a frozen ball will dictate whether you (a) hit the object ball first, then the cushion; (b) hit the cushion and then the object ball; or (c) hit both cushion and object ball simultaneously. If, for example, you need to send the cue ball around the table after pocketing the shot, you'll benefit from hitting the object ball first, rather than the cushion. Hitting the cushion first will slow down your cue ball and force it off the shot sideways, no matter the spin you've placed on it. Refer to figure 3.4 for an example of cue ball position after a frozen ball shot hit "object ball first" versus the reaction of the cue ball if you've hit "rail first."

BANK SHOTS

If you've spent time around the game and have had the opportunity to see some of the better players play, you've probably heard the phrase, "banks are open." It's a form of flattery offered to a player for consistently pocketing top-shelf bank shots. If you want to earn such flattery for your own banking talents, you'll require knowledge in two areas: the variables that affect a bank shot (including speed, spin, and angles) and a banking "system" that works for you.

Speed and Spin

Figure 3.5 shows the Goldilocks version of speed variables in banking. Shot A has been hit too hard. The object ball will rebound at a sharp angle and come up short of the pocket. Shot B has been hit too soft, and the object ball has missed the pocket on the other side. Shot C is just right—hit firm but not hard, dropping dead center into the pocket. This happens for two reasons. First, on a harder shot, the rubber in the cushion will compress, forcing the ball out at a sharper angle than that at which it approached the cushion. Second,

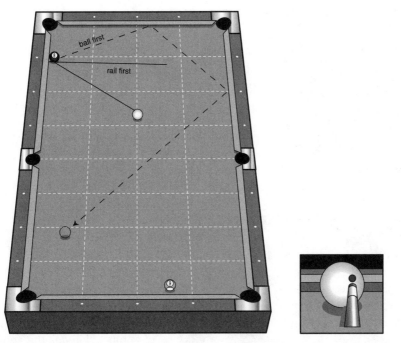

ball first

rail first

Figure 3.4 In this shot, hitting the object ball before the rail will allow you to play position on the nine ball.

the object ball will be skidding, not rolling, after contact with the cushion. Conversely, a shot hit too softly will roll into and away from the cushion, causing it to "go long."

Figure 3.6 illustrates the same three shots, but this time, the variable has changed from speed to spin. In shot C, the object ball has come up short because left-hand english was used on the cue ball, which put right-hand english on the object ball (remember the gear effect?). Shot B used right-hand english on the cue ball, resulting in left-hand english on the object ball, so the object ball traveled farther right, too long for its intended destination. Shot A employed a center ball hit, again, perfect in this instance.

While this certainly makes a case for the medium-speed, center ball hit, you don't always have that luxury when faced with a bank shot, so these variables then become useful tools. Figure 3.7 shows two shots that have little chance of crossing the table into the corner pocket with a medium-stroked, center ball hit. However, knowing the variables of speed and spin, you can execute the shot with low inside english and greater force. This will effectively reduce the angle at which the object ball rebounds from the cushion.

For the shot in figure 3.8, you are attempting to bank the shot very softly so the cue ball drifts gently to the rail for another shot. You should use running english to "close" the angle coming off the object ball that you open up with the soft roll.

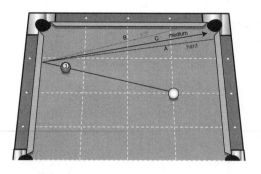

Figure 3.5 The speed of the ball changes angles at which the ball will bank. Greater speeds produce sharper angles.

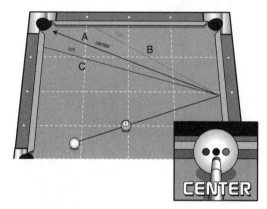

Figure 3.6 Notice how the use of english changes the angle of rebound from the cushion.

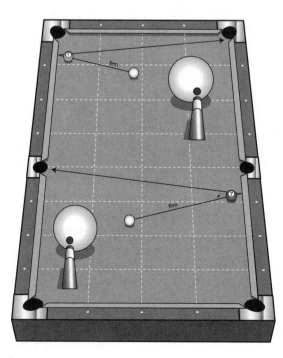

Figure 3.7 Using low, inside english allows you to shorten the natural angle the object balls would take if hit full by the cue ball.

Angle

The other variables you should concern yourself with on bank shots are the angles of attack, including the angle from the cue ball to the object ball, and from the object ball to the cushion.

Figure 3.9 illustrates a crossover bank, meaning your cue ball must cross over the natural angle of the bank shot. As the cue ball does so, it will hit the object ball on the right-hand side and impart sidespin on it, causing the ball to rebound at a wider angle than that at which it entered the cushion. If you can't see the cue ball go directly into the corner pocket, as shown by the "kiss" line in the diagram, you should not attempt a bank shot because you will get that dreaded double kiss. The cue ball on the right does have a clear line to the pocket so it will *not* be involved in the double kiss. This principle holds true for all cross-corner or straight-back shots banked off one rail.

Figure 3.10 shows the opposite situation, where you are shooting away from the bank angle of the object ball. This shot, because you'll hit away from the angle of attack, will naturally put inside english on the object ball, forcing it to rebound from the cushion at a sharper angle.

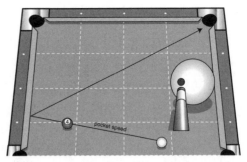

Figure 3.8 The use of spin allows you to hit this shot with less speed.

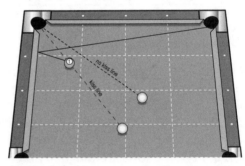

Figure 3.9 Cross-over banks are possible when you can see the cue ball travel directly to the corner pocket without interference.

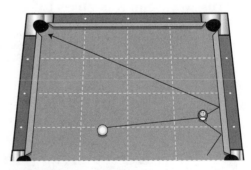

Figure 3.10 Shooting a bank shot away from the angle of attack.

These shots demonstrate the effect of collision-induced sidespin on the object ball from the cue ball. But this sidespin also occurs with the object ball's angle of attack to the cushion. The angles between 20 and 60 degrees pick up the most collision-induced sidespin. After about 60 degrees, the more severe the angle, the less sidespin is picked up by the object ball. For example, a cross-side bank with very little angle will not pick up much english rebounding off the cushion.

Banking Systems

Now that you've seen how different variables can determine how you play a bank shot, it's time to discuss two systems that will help develop your consistency in pocketing bank shots. Keep in mind, as you learn and utilize these systems, that bank shots are still primarily a matter of getting to know the reactions of the cue ball and object ball, paying attention to the angles in and out from the cushions, and good old-fashioned memory work. Once you've had a chance to practice your bank shots, the greatest advice we can give you is to treat the bank shot like any other shot. Too many players get caught up in making the bank shot. But if you focus simply on pocketing the ball on your way to your next shot, you'll be mindful of position play on the cue ball, follow through more smoothly, and execute more often.

Mirror Image

The most common banking system employed by players is the mirror image. If you practice with a partner and have a mirror large enough to hold up next to the table, you'll get a striking visual example of how this system works. But most players don't. The mirror image system works anyway, because you can use your imagination to create the image.

Figure 3.11 shows an imaginary table placed next to a real table. By aiming the ball on the real table directly at the side pocket on the imaginary table, you will successfully bank the ball cross side into the intended pocket. Obviously, you'll need to take into consideration all the variables we've already discussed, but this technique is a great way to quickly visualize the spot on the cushion to aim your object ball at for a perfect bank.

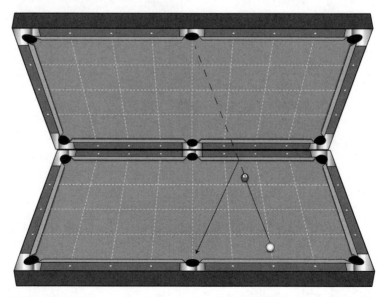

Figure 3.11 The most common way to become familiar with banks is the mirror image system.

Spin It In

Figure 3.12 illustrates an example of the "spin it in" banking technique. As you'll note from the cue ball position and angle of attack from the cue ball to the object ball, you'll line up for a fuller hit on the object ball than you'd aim for using the mirror image system. Then, you use left-hand english to throw the object ball to the right into the correct spot on the cushion to rebound back to the pocket. This system requires that you know the spot where the object ball must contact the cushion in order to rebound back into a pocket.

Let's take this a step further with another pro secret to spinning banks. Many legendary bank players would actually rather bank balls using inside english. Using inside english transfers english to the object ball. This allows a banked ball to bounce off the cushion at a more shallow angle. In figure 3.13, a center ball hit is shown for a bank shot, along with a hit using inside english to pocket the ball. Note how the english allows a more shallow angle to the pocket. This also takes side-spin off the object ball to give you a truer roll.

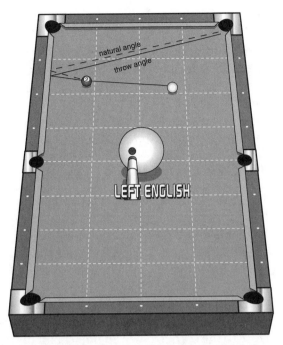

Figure 3.12 "Spinning" in a bank with left english.

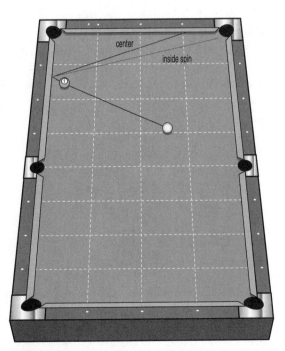

Figure 3.13 Inside spin allows you to cleanly pocket this bank shot.

KICK SHOTS

The kick shot is similar to the bank shot in that a cushion is needed to perform the shot. But rather than using the cue ball to send an object ball into the cushion and out again, you'll be sending the cue ball directly into the cushion, intending for it to rebound off and contact an object ball. This section will develop your kicking skills on common one-rail kicks. For information on multiple-rail kicks, refer to chapter 4.

Defensive Kick Shots

The most common use of the kick shot is in defensive play—sending the cue ball into a rail and back out to contact an object ball you couldn't hit directly. We'll talk more about defensive kick shots in the next chapter, but before you get there, you should develop your kicking skills.

The mirror image system of banking is easily adapted to the one-rail kick. To get a feel for the kick shot, begin practice without the use of an object ball. Aim the cue ball into the rail, attempting to bank it into the opposite corner or opposite side pocket. Once you've become proficient at getting the cue ball close to the corner, place an object ball in the cue ball's path to the pocket and see if you consistently hit that. Remember to aim the cue ball at the contact point on the object ball.

When the angle is wider than 45 degrees, you have to adjust your aiming slightly (as in the bank shot) to take into account the cue ball picking up sidespin from the collision with the rail. Plenty of pros use just a touch of inside english when kicking one rail, which allows the cue ball to "flatten out" its angle off the rail, sending it back to the intended object ball on a more natural rolling path.

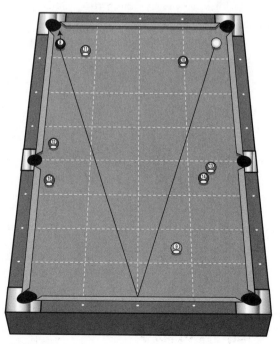

Offensive Kick Shots

The other use of a kick shot is in offensive play, but this is a top-shelf shot that is often overlooked. Note the example shown in figure 3.14. You're in a heated game of 8-Ball, and your opponent has blocked the

Figure 3.14 A well-played kick shot can win games.

eight ball with his balls. By performing an offensive one-rail kick, and calling the eight ball you'll not only get the hit, you can win the game.

COMBINATIONS

A combination shot requires you to shoot the cue ball into an object ball, which then sends a second (or third) object ball into the pocket. This top-shelf shot comes up more often than you'd think and becomes easier once you get the hang of it.

In the combination shot examples shown in figure 3.15, two object balls are frozen together, and they are not quite in line to the pocket. If these shots were hit full, you would miss the target ball, as shown.

Here's where most players would assume that they need to aim the cue ball farther to the right (for shot at right) to pocket the ball. Wrong. Contact the seven ball on the opposite side instead to throw the second ball to the pocket, as shown. Keep in mind, the farther the shot is from the pocket, the more you can alter the path of the object ball.

In combination shots where the object balls aren't frozen, your chances of pocketing the second ball increase as the distance between the two object balls, and the distance between the object ball and the pocket, decreases. In figure 3.16, shot A is a very makeable combination, as the two object balls are close together, and the target object ball is close to the pocket. Shot B however, though it appears relatively simple, has too much distance between the two object balls and is farther from the pocket. This is a lower-percentage shot. Shot C offers a difficult shot from the cue ball to the first object ball, but since the target object ball is close to the pocket, it's in the medium difficulty range.

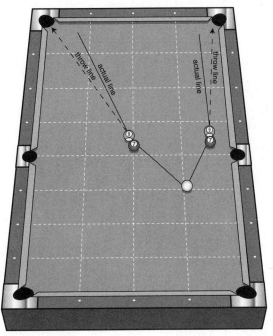

Figure 3.15 Frozen ball combinations pocketed with the use of "throw."

Now let's talk about how to actually pocket a combination shot. One trick players find helpful is to aim at the rail beyond the shot. Once you line up toward the hit on the first object ball, aim right through the ball to the point beyond it on the cushion. This will help you to stay down on the shot and

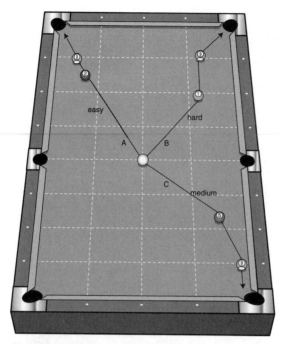

Figure 3.16 The greater the distance between the target ball and the pocket, the tougher the shot.

visualize the whole shot without trying to actually look at each ball during execution, which becomes tricky when multiple balls are in play.

Another hint is to create an imaginary pocket for the first object ball. By pretending the second object ball is a pocket, you'll have less of a tendency to look too far ahead on the shot. Most players employ the ghost ball theory of aiming on combination shots (this method is described in the chapter on aiming), because it's easiest to visualize the cue ball sending the object ball to a ghost ball position on the target ball.

Having said that, it's worth mentioning a few tricky variables. If you are cutting the first ball to the right to make the combination, you will put left english on your first object ball naturally (collision-induced throw). Hit the ball firmer and the shot will incur less spin, increasing your chance of success. The most successful combination shot experts hit these top-shelf shots firm, but not too hard, with plenty of confidence.

You're also better off trying to keep the hit on your cue ball as close to center as possible. The use of english magnifies the variables. There are players and teachers who believe you should use outside english to "straighten out" or take the spin off your first object ball. There's a lot to be said for this, but less-experienced players too often have a tendency to overdo it. If you would like to experiment with this method, don't use more than a one-quarter to one-half tip of english. Your goal is only to take the sidespin off the first object ball before it hits the second object ball. Abundant use of english won't accomplish that goal. Note: When using english, you'll also have to hit the combination a bit fuller than you think.

Finally, plan on where the first ball in the combination will go, particularly in relation to where the cue ball will go, to avoid position play trouble. No sense in getting hooked, regardless of how fine a combination shot you execute. If your object ball is hanging in the pocket, consider making both balls (the ball in the pocket and the ball you are shooting into it). To do this, simply use draw on the cue ball. This puts topspin on the contact object ball and causes it to follow the target ball right into the pocket.

Hitting Hangers

Your opponent hangs the object ball in the pocket, and you rush to the table, only to end up terribly out of line on the next shot. How could this happen?

It's easier than you might think. Players often get lazy with a hanger and forget to have a destination for the cue ball in mind. Also, the object ball is so close to the pocket that if the cue ball makes any kind of contact with it at all, the ball will fall. But you'd better be precise as to where you want to hit the object ball, *especially* when you can hit it anywhere at all.

Figure 3.17 illustrates three of the many destinations just waiting for your cue ball. The object ball is hanging in the upper left-hand corner, and the cue ball

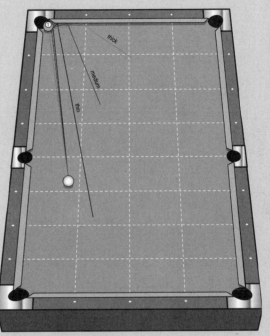

Figure 3.17 Three destinations for the cue ball.

is about a diamond in from the same side near the center of the table. For your first exercise, try to hit all these shots at the same speed:

1. A thin hit with center ball will bring your cue ball out to the position indicated by the line labeled thin.

2. A half-ball hit gives the cue ball a wider angle coming off the short rail, carrying the cue ball to the position indicated by the line labeled medium.

3. Finally, a thicker hit opens up the angle off the object ball, taking the cue ball to about the first diamond on the short rail before it rebounds to the position shown by the line labeled thick.

CAROMS

Figure 3.18 Pocketing a target ball with the use of a helper ball; called a carom shot.

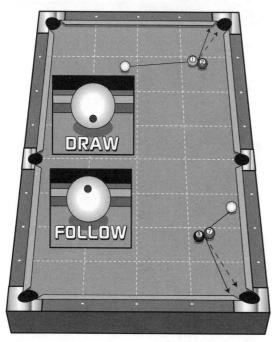

Figure 3.19 Using draw and follow to influence the tangent line in frozen ball carom shots.

Similar to the combination shot, the carom shot also employs the use of an object ball to pocket another object ball. But instead of using the object ball to pocket your target ball, your target object ball will bump into the "helper" object ball, allowing the target ball to change its normal path and head into the pocket. It's not a difficult top-shelf shot if you know how to line up a carom properly.

Figure 3.18 shows a simple carom shot. The object ball is shot into the helper ball, glancing off it on the tangent line and being sent neatly into the pocket. To know what spot on the helper ball you must contact with your intended object ball, line up the outside of the pocket with the edge of the helper ball as indicated. This is the point you'll want to aim your target ball, because using the outside pocket edge as an aiming point compensates for the aim versus contact point dilemma.

Speed and spin are variables that can confuse things in the execution of a carom shot, or in some instances, they can be valuable tools. Try this same shot using different speeds and cue tip placements to discover how the angles off the helper ball will change. If the target ball is sliding into the helper ball from a hard hit, the angle coming off will be wider than if it's rolling. That means a thinner hit is required for a shot using greater force, and a fuller hit is needed for a soft, slow shot.

In a frozen ball carom shot (see figure 3.19), you can use draw or follow to influence the tangent line and subsequent path of your object ball. Using draw will push the object ball forward, allowing you to extend the tangent line from where it would normally hit on the cushion, and sending the object ball to the pocket instead. Likewise, using follow can bring the object ball back off the tangent line. By experimenting with these shots, you'll be able to learn how much you can alter a tangent line with the use of draw, follow, and different cue stick speeds.

THE BILLIARD SHOT

Like a carom shot, a billiard shot uses an object ball as a helper, but a billiard shot sends the cue ball directly into the helper ball so that the cue ball glances off the tangent line to pocket the target ball. The example in figure 3.20 shows you how advantageous this shot might be in a game such as 9-Ball, where you are required to contact the lowest-numbered ball on the table first. When you send the cue ball into the first ball, it will naturally glance off and pocket the nine, winning the game! The principle for aiming the billiard is the same as the carom shot, and today many folks refer to either shot as a carom. Using inside english can also make this shot easier. With a center ball hit, you will pick up outside spin, but using a touch of inside english will "throw" the ball back toward its target.

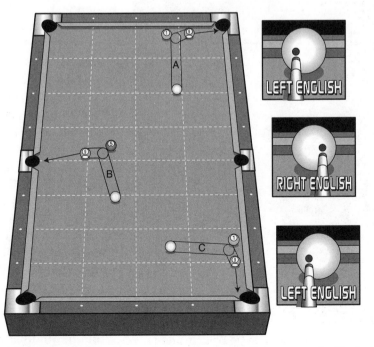

Figure 3.20 In each of the shots shown, the cue ball is caromed off a helper ball to pocket the target ball.

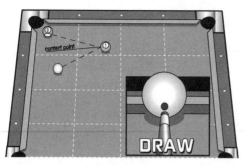

Figure 3.21 Changing the natural angle the cue ball would take off the helper ball with draw.

You don't always need a perfect tangent line to carom the cue ball into another ball. For the shot shown in figure 3.21, you can draw the cue ball off the helper ball (as if you were attempting to scratch) and send it neatly into the nine ball for a game-winning billiard shot. To judge this shot, you "split the difference," meaning you contact the helper ball at the midway point between the cue ball and object ball, as illustrated.

JUMP SHOTS

Today's durable pool equipment, including the ultratough phenolic resin balls that replaced ivory and the slate table beds that replaced early wooden models, makes it more practical than ever to take to the air with a top-shelf jump shot. But without knowledge of how and when to perform this shot, you just might hurt yourself (or an innocent bystander).

Sending the cue ball airborne over a ball to hit your intended object ball is not as difficult as you'd expect. The first thing you must do is change your stance. Turn your feet almost sideways toward the direction of the shot so you can elevate the butt end of your cue. With the sideways stance, the cue stick can move freely through the shot without your body getting in the way. Your stance should also be elevated for this shot. Figure 3.22 shows 2002 BCA Open 9-Ball champion Charlie Williams in an ideal jump stance.

Figure 3.22 Pro player Charlie Williams demonstrates winning jump shot form.

Carom or Combination?

We've seen many a player try to position the cue ball for a combination, when the easier and smarter shot would have been to cinch the shot at hand and play easy shape for a carom. Most overlook the carom shot because they have little confidence in it. But there are distinct advantages in playing a carom over a combination. First and foremost, the carom may be the easier shot. Second, a carom shot will allow you to put a lot of distance between the cue ball and the object ball after the shot. These are great opportunities for two-way shots, that is, both a defensive and offensive play.

However, you should never play a shot without considering all the movement it drives. Will the first ball be driven to a rail, into a cluster, in front of a pocket? Where will the cue ball end up in relation to the first ball? Can this be controlled, manipulated, or altered? You need to control the "helper" ball as well as the cue ball. Choose the right speed and angle, and think the whole shot through before execution.

In the situation shown in figure 3.23, you might think the next shot (after pocketing the two ball) is to play a combination on the nine ball using the three ball. However, pocketing the two ball in the lower corner pocket and trying to move the cue ball up and down the table with follow, or trying to draw it back with power, would make the two ball shot very difficult.

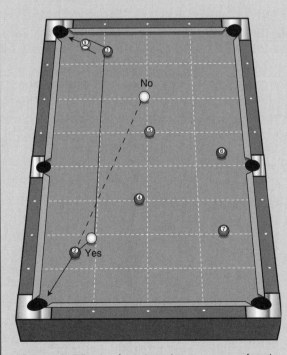

Figure 3.23 In this situation a carom shot is a better option than a combination.

The better shot in this situation is to cinch the two ball. Using a below center hit, the cue ball will slide over naturally. From here it's a relatively easy shot to carom the cue ball off the three to make the nine in the corner. If, by some fluke, you don't pocket the nine, the cue ball will come to rest in the immediate area of the nine ball. The three ball, if hit with medium speed, will come to rest at the other end of the table. The beauty of this shot is that even if you miss the carom, your opponent will probably have a tougher shot, and you'll have another opportunity at the table.

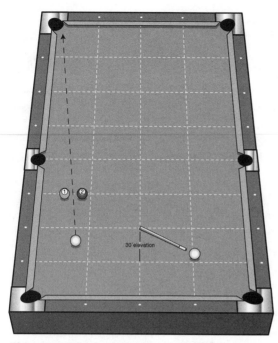

Figure 3.24 Set up this simple drill to practice your jump shot skills.

When first attempting to jump a ball, players often elevate the butt end of the cue too high. Note from the figure the relaxed elevation of the cue. Remember, you're just trying to skip the cue ball along the table. You are in fact shooting the cue ball into the bed of the table so that it bounces back up and over an impediment. The closer the interfering ball is to the cue ball, the steeper the angle of attack on the cue ball (too steep an angle will "trap" the cue ball between the table surface and your cue stick, preventing the cue ball from bouncing back up from the slate).

To get familiar with the jump shot, use a piece of chalk as the obstruction between the cue ball and object ball. Place the chalk about 12 inches from the cue ball, and put an object ball in front of a pocket. Raise the butt end of your cue about 20 to 30 degrees. As your head is raised for this shot, so is the face of the cue ball.

Now it's time to increase the challenge. Place two object balls less than a ball's width apart with the gap facing a corner pocket, as indicated in figure 3.24. Using these two balls as your obstruction, place the cue ball anywhere from 12 to 18 inches away and jump over the gap between the two balls. You'll notice it doesn't take much to jump the edges of balls (see figure 3.25), which is what you are doing when the cue ball travels airborne between them. You're jumping over the edge, not the whole ball. In other words, since both your cue ball and the interfering balls are round, if the cue ball is just slightly higher at the moment they pass each other, their edges won't touch.

Time for the moment of truth, the full-ball jump! A little secret before you attempt a full-ball jump: Never look at the ball you intend to jump over. You must

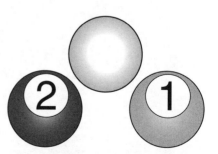

Figure 3.25 Jumping over balls doesn't always require the cue ball to clear the entire ball, as shown by this cue ball clearing the edges of two balls.

look at the spot where you want the cue ball to arrive, just as in any other shot. Not aiming toward the object ball you intend to hit will produce poor results. Once you've sighted your shot, you're ready. You'll need more force for this shot, but not much more leverage on the back of your cue stick (again, you want to avoid trapping the cue ball).

With so many gadgets on the market, you can also take advantage of technology to improve your jumping skills. Use a jump cue if you're allowed to do so where you play. Jump cues are built solely for this purpose; weight is taken from the back end of the cue stick to allow an easier "pop" into the cue ball with the cue tip.

There are plenty of ways a jump shot can be used, but let's stay focused on the five uses that offer the highest percentage of success:

1. The cue ball jumps over the edge of an interfering ball to reach the target object ball, as shown in figure 3.25.

2. The cue ball jumps to hit an object ball above its equator, then continues to rise to clear interfering balls for better resulting cue ball position (see figure 3.26).

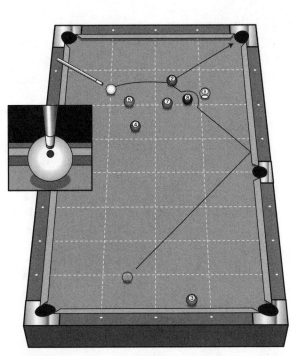

3. Cue ball jumps fully over an impeding ball to reach and pocket target object ball. (Fig. 3.27, shot A)

4. The cue ball jumps to hit the first object ball above its equator, causing the object ball to leave the bed of the table and hop over the edge of an interfering ball (see figure 3.27, shot B).

Figure 3.26 Jumping the cue ball over interfering balls after contact with the object ball.

5. The cue ball jumps into the cushion, clearing an interfering ball on the rebound (see figure 3.28).

Practice every type of jump shot until you are comfortable with each one, and then pack them all in your bag of tricks for actual game situations.

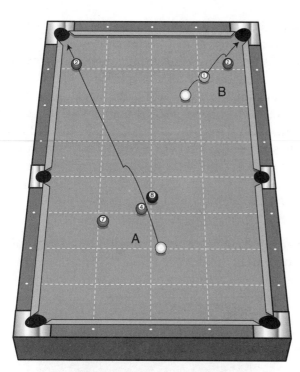

Figure 3.27 In shot A, the cue ball jumps a full ball. In shot B, the cue ball forces the object ball to jump over an interfering ball.

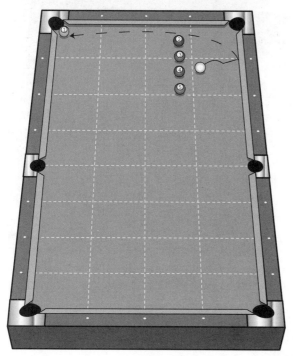

Figure 3.28 The cue ball jumps into the cushion and clears an interfering ball on the rebound (a popular trick shot).

CURVE SHOTS

Our final top-shelf shot is another physics-defying beauty. Rather than defying gravity to leap over impeding balls like the jump shot, the curve shot defies the physics of forward motion, allowing you to curve the cue ball around impeding balls. Just as you elevated the clock face for the jump shot, you should do so for the curve shot, and again, you should elevate your stance and the butt end of the cue stick. Figure 3.29 illustrates your challenges—to clear impeding balls on both sides of the table using a curve shot. Note in each shot the position of your cue tip. To curve around the balls on the left, you'll be using low left english, and on the right, low right english. Begin by shooting soft, slowly increasing your force with practice. As you'll quickly discover, it doesn't take much force to produce a curving path for the cue ball.

A full massé shot is the extreme curve shot that can send the cue ball up and back toward you without ever hitting another ball or cushion. This shot is seldom used in tournament play and is reserved for those with an interest in trick shots and fancy shots. For that reason, we have not included it in this text. If you want to learn to master this shot without hurting the equipment, or yourself, you might want to find a qualified local house pro or instructor to offer you hands-on guidance.

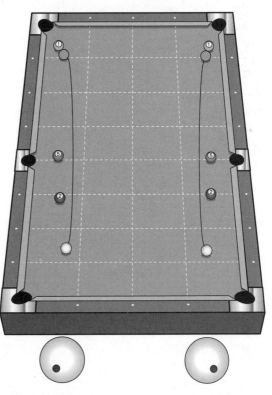

Figure 3.29 Curve shots allow us to change the straight line path from the cue ball to the object ball.

So, have you found your own favorite top-shelf shot yet? Even if you have, remember our earlier warning. A bit of practice devoted to each of these top-shelf shots will provide you with a greater arsenal of knowledge and skill at the table.

Mapping the Table

4

Okay, so you've made it through the refresher course on body position and aiming. You've worked on your top-shelf shots. Now it's time to talk strategy. Strategy is more than just thinking one pocket at a time. You have to think of this ball, and the next, and the next. This chapter will teach the many ways to look beyond the current situation so that you can strategize your run-out (or slick defensive move) based on the best shots, not a stroke of good luck!

Once you've established sound fundamentals and the ability to pocket a ball, the next areas of your game to be developed are your offensive and defensive strategies, including position play, resulting patterns, safeties, and returning safeties. Here's where pool gets really fun! Staying at the table, or getting back to the table with a well-played safety, allows you to spend more of your time playing and less time watching your opponent run out.

POSITIONS, EVERYBODY!

Playing position simply means planning where you want the cue ball to arrive following your current shot in order to be in the best position to make your next shot, and each shot afterward. Position play strings together your individual shots for run-outs. Run-outs win games.

To play good position, you'll need to control your cue ball, and you'll need to learn a few key ways to send the cue ball around the table for your next shot when the situation requires it. Key position plays can be classified by how many cushions will be contacted in the process of playing position.

Look Ma, No Rails!

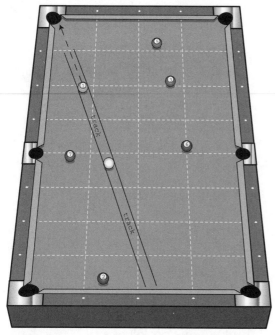

Figure 4.1 "No rail" position offers predictability; you can place the cue ball anywhere on the track shown.

No rail position shots include most straight-in stop shots and straight-in (or nearly straight-in) shots using a bit of draw or follow. The advantages to such shots include less distance traveled and a relatively predictable outcome—the cue ball will stay on a line similar to its path to the object ball. This is illustrated in figure 4.1. Shooting in the one ball, you know the cue ball can travel anywhere on the line shown to get position on a variety of other balls on the table. On the downside, if you are shooting at the two ball next, you will prefer to have an angle to get to it. Now you're forced to use extreme draw. Working on your position play using no rails is very good practice for control of your cue ball, but in most games, you'll need more.

One Rail

One-rail position is so common, and so often used, it's impossible to imagine all the possibilities, let alone illustrate them. Virtually all off-angle shots within a foot of any cushion on the table will require the cue ball to travel into—and back out from—the rail after contact with the object ball. It cannot be avoided, and in most cases, you won't want to avoid it, since you can use that cushion (with whatever spin you've put on your cue ball) to arrive comfortably at your next shot. But what's equally important to know is that even though one-rail position is both useful and extremely common, it may not be your best option.

Two Rails

Two-rail position is an excellent way to get shape on your next shot, especially when you wish to take speed off the cue ball or change the angle of approach of the cue ball into or away from your next shot. Figure 4.2 shows an example of this. Shot A indicates the correct shot, while shot B shows how players might try for one-rail position and subsequently cross over the line of attack of the shot or sacrifice accuracy.

The importance of the two-rail shot cannot be overstated. It's easy to identify less knowledgeable players by how many rails they use on most shots. Experienced players know how to use the rails to their advantage. Inexperienced players, or those who have never been taught the subtleties of the game, will use predominantly no rail and one-rail position plays. Learning the common two-rail tracks that the cue ball will take after contact with the object ball requires practice and observation. To get started, set up an off-angle shot into the corner pocket. Your goal is for the cue ball, after contact with the object ball, to be sent into the short rail, then long rail, and then back to the center of the table. Examples are illustrated in figure 4.3. As you learn these tracks, you'll be better able to predict the cue ball's path around the table. This will help you avoid common errors such as scratching in the side pocket from the short rail (we see this one a lot!).

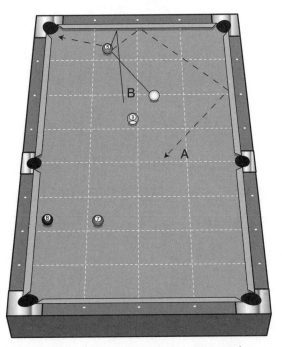

Figure 4.2 In this situation, the two-rail position is the best option.

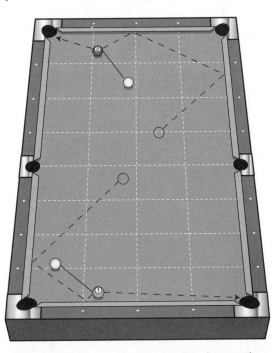

Figure 4.3 Learning short rail to long rail to table center tracks will improve your position play.

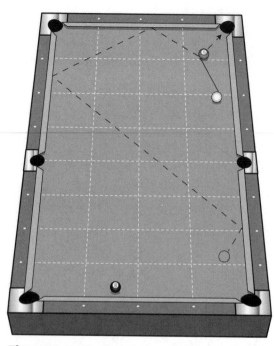

Figure 4.4 Getting three rail position from the five ball to the eight ball.

Three Rails

Less common, but equally important, are three-rail shots for position. While contacting three rails with the cue ball may sound complicated, it's actually a natural position play for many shots. Figure 4.4 shows a shot on the five ball. It would be awkward to shoot this one rail or two rails, but a natural three-rail shot puts you in perfect position for the eight ball.

You can often turn two-rail shots into three-rail shots when contacting the third rail will get you closer to your intended target. This is useful, so long as contact with the third rail keeps the cue ball coming into the angle of attack for your next shot without crossing over it. An example is shown in figure 4.5.

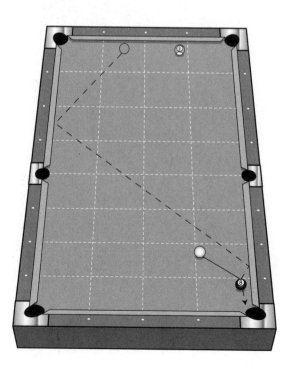

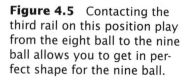

Figure 4.5 Contacting the third rail on this position play from the eight ball to the nine ball allows you to get in perfect shape for the nine ball.

Four or More

Yes, four-rail position shots can also come into play, though these are rare. Figure 4.6 offers an example of when you might contact four rails to get back in position for a shot on the nine ball. You've been left on the wrong side of the eight to get on the nine ball easily after pocketing the eight, so sending the cue ball around the table and back for a shot on the nine could require four rails, as shown.

What's important to note in all these rail position plays is that knowing the "tracks" the cue ball takes around the table allows you to easily predict the path of the cue ball as it rebounds off multiple cushions.

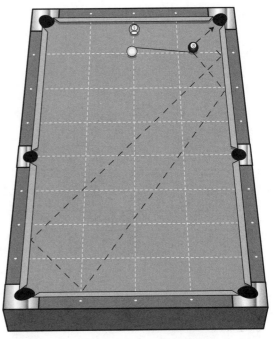

Figure 4.6 Four-rail position can come in handy when you're left with bad position on the next shot, as shown.

Position Patterns

These position plays are grouped into patterns, which you'll recognize easily as you play and practice more often. The most common patterns for simple position play come in three flavors: working balls close together (usually at one end of the table), working the balls from one end of the table to the other end, and working back and forth between both ends of the table.

When working at one end of the table, as shown in figure 4.7, you have the advantage of

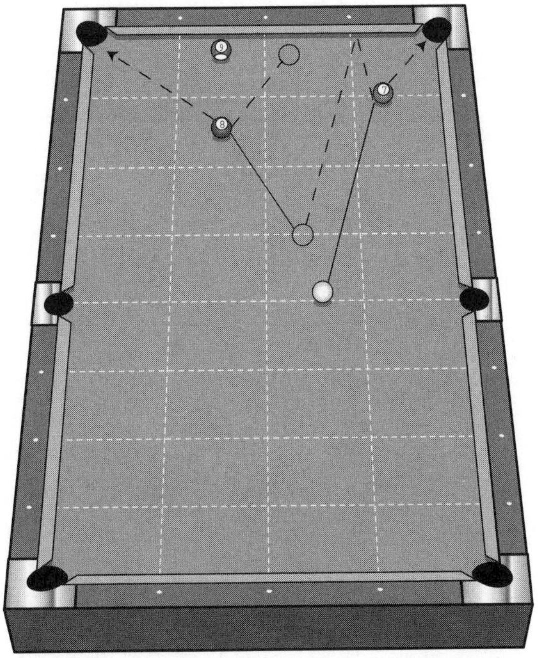

Figure 4.7 Working position play at one end of the table.

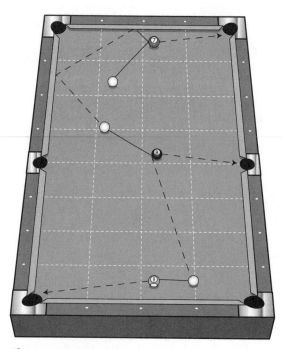

Figure 4.8 Working position play from one end of the table to the other.

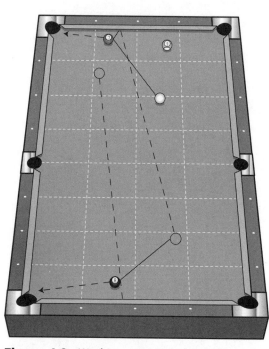

Figure 4.9 Working position play back and forth between both ends of the table.

not having to move the cue ball very far (less distance equals less chance for error). But you will also be under the gun to keep the cue ball on the correct side of the ball, lest you have to send the cue ball up and down the table to get back on the next shot. In the pattern shown in figure 4.8, you need to work the balls from one end of the table to the other, pocketing what can be pocketed on one end, moving to the side, and then down to the other end of the table. Finally, figure 4.9 shows an example of working the balls back and forth between both ends of the table. In this 9-Ball diagram, the seven and nine balls are on one end of the table, and the eight on the other end, so you're forced to move the cue ball a greater distance to achieve the run-out.

LAWS OF PATTERN PLAY

Solid pattern play begins with knowing how to plan ahead. Throw the one, two, and three balls out on the table, along with your cue ball. Let them come to rest anywhere. Now, take the cue ball and place it in the most advantageous spot to pocket the one, get shape on the two, and make the two with resulting shape on the three.

You've just performed a three-ball pattern play, thinking two balls ahead from the first shot (the one ball) to the last (the three ball). As any professional player will be quick to point out, this is the *least* amount of planning you should do on any shot during a game—a pro is always thinking at least two shots ahead, usually three or four.

Why? Let's look at an example. Figure 4.10 shows what should be a simple three-ball pattern. Put the cue ball behind the one, stop the cue ball for a straight-in shot at the two—oops—how will you get on the three? Now, look at figure 4.11. By knowing you have to get to the three ball (thinking two balls ahead), you can choose a better shot on the one, that is, a shot that will give you the angle on the two necessary to get over to the three ball. As you progress through the rack, so will your three-ball pattern. In other words, once you're on the two ball, you'll play position for the three to then get on the four. When you arrive at the three, you'll be looking at how to shoot the three to get to the four in a way that will enable you to reach the five, and so on, through the entire rack. Pattern play isn't just an important part of pool; it's mandatory if you want to continue making more than two balls in a row. The following laws of pattern play will have you planning a run-out in no time.

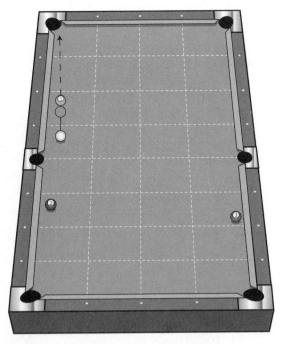

Figure 4.10 A simple three ball pattern, made difficult without angles.

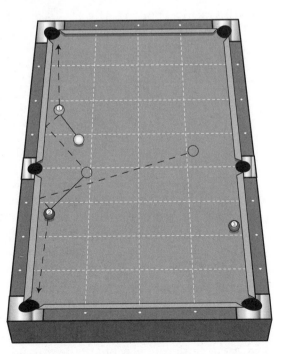

Figure 4.11 The same three ball pattern, made easy with angles.

Map It Out

In most games, especially today's most popular games of 8-Ball and 9-Ball, the table will guide your pattern play, though 8-Ball, because you have a choice of which ball to shoot, will offer more options. It's your job to listen to what the table is telling you. Here's just a few of the things to listen for, using three 9-Ball racks as examples:

- This rack is an easy run if you draw the cue ball back on the one ball. The rest of the rack will be simple stop shots. You don't have to move the cue ball much at all. Doing so will put you at peril.

- This rack will take some planning. The key ball is the three. If you can get to the correct side of the four after the three, you can easily run this rack.

- This rack can't be run. There are so many balls tied up and clumped together that you're looking at a safety battle. Making the first ball or two that is clear can't get you to a comfortable spot to break up the clumps. Opt for a safety.

Vivian Villarreal, the "Texas Tornado," checks her position play options.

By simply looking ahead and drawing a mental map of each table layout, you'll quickly know if you have a workable run-out, a tricky pattern play, or a situation that will require a safety battle. Conversely, if you simply begin pocketing balls, which is possible in each rack, you'll run into trouble rather quickly.

Right Side/Wrong Side

Amateur players seldom understand why the professionals obsess over getting on the wrong side of the ball. Simply put, being on the wrong side, while still possible to work your way out of the situation, puts you at a huge disadvantage to continue a run. The right (correct) side of any position play offers you the

A Game Winner

Keeping your cool at the table in pressure situations can be handier than you think. In the shot illustrated, your opponent thinks he has left you safe, with his remaining ball blocking the eight ball's path to the corner pocket.

Maintain your composure and execute the game-winning shot by calling the eight in the corner (figure 4.12), slow rolling it to the rail, and letting it dribble into the pocket. The pocket is bigger than you think it is! Note: You can only cheat the pocket in this manner if you hit this shot softly. A hard hit will send the eight ball spitting out at a sharper angle from the cushion and missing the corner.

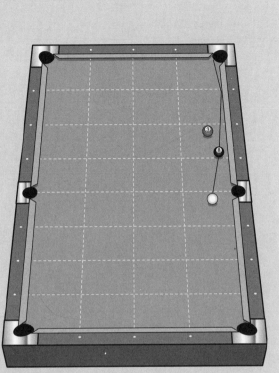

Figure 4.12 The eight-ball does a slow roll to rail, dribbling into the pocket.

easiest, most natural path to the next shot and to get in line for the shot after that, and so on. Getting on the wrong side means you're now in the position of having to do something "funny" to get to the correct side of the next shot. It also means you'll have to move the cue ball around more. This could force you to move other object balls, which in turn forces you to rethink your position play mid-rack. These are all run-out percentage killers.

In the example shown in figure 4.13, the cue ball has landed on the wrong side of the three ball. If it had landed in the shaded area, a run-out would be probable. Instead, you'll have to fight your way back to get on the four ball and hope the cue ball doesn't collide with the six and seven balls. Keep in mind that it's often better to give yourself a longer shot with the correct angle than to risk trying to be too close and getting on the wrong side of the ball.

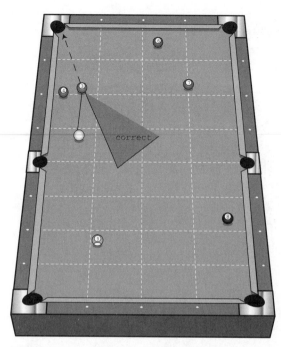

Figure 4.13 The best position for the cue ball to the three ball (shaded area).

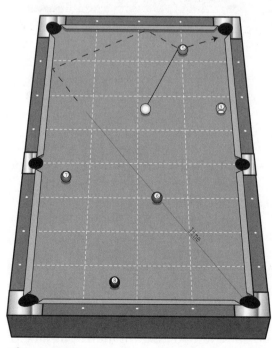

Figure 4.14 Using two rails to come into the angle of attack.

There's even less room for error when playing position on a side pocket shot. Getting on the wrong side of a side pocket shot will force you to send the cue ball all the way around the table to get back in line. Famed player and instructor Buddy Hall goes so far as to pretend that there are no side pockets on a table and plays position on the corner pockets whenever possible.

Beware the Attack Line

Crossing over the line is a difficult concept for many players to understand. The line of attack is the line from the pocket, through the object ball, and extending across the table, as shown in figure 4.14. The shot shown in this diagram further illustrates this concept. By coming into the angle of the shot on the six ball from your previous shot on the five, you have a very good chance of getting on the correct side of the seven, to then get position on the eight ball.

Figure 4.15 shows another example, this time going away from the line of attack, rather than crossing it. Heading into, or away from, the angle of attack offers you the best opportunity to be in line for your next shot. Even if your speed control is off, with a shot hit slightly too soft or too hard, you'll still be on the proper side of the ball to get to your next shot.

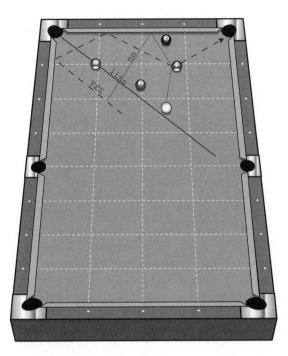

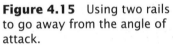

Figure 4.15 Using two rails to go away from the angle of attack.

Angles for Options

If you've seen players who consistently end up with straight-in shots that force them to cheat the pocket to create an angle to get on the next ball, you can surmise that those players are thinking one ball ahead. Sure, they got perfect shape on the next shot, but now what?

Unless you have a picture-perfect "stop-out" requiring nothing but stop shots through the entire rack (a pool player's dream, but seldom a reality!), you'll need those angles to open up your options to get on the next ball. Giving yourself an angle offers a multitude of options.

THINKING IT THROUGH

Now that you've learned position and pattern play, let's spruce things up with some mental tricks. Keeping these in the back of your mind as you play will allow you to visualize easier position plays and aid you in mapping your table situation.

Think Backward

Thinking backward is planning ahead in reverse, and it is an ideal strategy for games like 8-Ball and 9-Ball because you begin with the game-winning ball and work back from there. In 8-Ball, you'll decide the best place to be to pocket the game ball, then you'll decide which ball will get you there the easiest, then which ball to get to that one, and so on through the rack. In

9-Ball, it's even easier. Where must you be on the eight to get to the nine? Where must you be on the seven to get to that spot on the eight? By thinking back from the desired end of your game, you can often see potential problems easier and adjust your plan from the beginning. Once you've made a backward map of your table, proceed by thinking three balls ahead through the rack.

Shrink the Table

There are times when mapping the table will seem overwhelming, especially when playing on unfamiliar equipment or bigger tables. But no matter what size table you practice on, by visualizing the table stopping six inches in from each cushion, you can effectively shrink the size of the area you play on and open up your position play options. Playing position from one cushion to another limits your options because you'll be forced to shoot high on the cue ball. Center ball, stop shots, and draw shots are nearly impossible with the cue ball resting against the cushion. Hint: If your cue ball lands on or near the cushions often, you'll know immediately that your speed control needs some work.

Get Centered

No matter how proficient your table-mapping skills, sometimes you just won't be sure where to head next. No worries, it happens to all players. But the best way to eliminate the doubt is to head for the center of the table. Whenever you're in trouble, think you're in trouble, or just plain don't know what to do next, the best place to have your cue ball arrive is at or near the center of the table. From the center you'll usually have more avenues available from the cue ball to other object balls, and it's generally an easy place to get to from most other places on the table. This also gives you an automatic destination for your cue ball when you're confused.

From the center of the table, you'll naturally have a shorter shot. With the cue ball in the center of the table, your next shot will never be more than a half table's length away, making it simpler to see and hit your next object ball. Being closer to the ball means you will probably be able to assume your normal stance and use your normal bridge. It also enables you to avoid the problems already discussed regarding getting stuck too close to a cushion.

Learning to maneuver your cue ball to the table's center is also a fantastic way to practice. Try shooting every shot with the intention of having your cue ball arrive back in the middle of the table. This exercise demands excellent cue ball control and will reward you with increased position play skills.

Don't Get Sideswiped

Naturally, if the layout of the table is such that the side pocket is an easy route to the next shot, use it. But if you have other options, there are two good table-mapping reasons why the corner pockets are more favorable than side pockets. First, the corner pocket has a larger target area. The rail arm extending from a corner pocket is about one and a half times the length of the rail arm extending from the side pocket. In addition, the angle at which the rail arm is extended from a corner pocket is more open, allowing it to be approached from many different positions on the table. The side pocket opening narrows at sharper angles of approach. When the target is generous, you have more angle choices; you can choose to aim at any part of the pocket that is available to you. This provides different angles and assists your positioning strategy (cheating the pocket). The closer the object ball is to the pocket, the more choices you have. In fact, when the ball is close enough, you can change a cut to the left into a cut to the right or go straight into a rail first!

Second, you are limited in a side pocket cut by the direction that the cue ball can take. If you have a left cut into the side pocket, the cue ball is going to the right half of the table whether you use center ball, draw, or follow. In a corner pocket, however, the simple choice of draw or follow can move the cue ball in opposite directions.

PLAYING IT SAFE

You may think most pros play an aggressive, offensive game that doesn't allow for much safety play, but in fact, the opposite is true. Many pros are known for having a very "tight" game, meaning they don't take chances; they play safe and let the other player make the mistakes.

Proper safety strategy includes knowing the types of safeties you can execute and knowing when it's best to play safe. In the sections on 8-Ball and 9-Ball, we'll offer actual match situations demonstrating safeties. But for now, let's focus on the types of safeties common in most games, how to execute them with success, and how to hone your safety strategy skills.

Cue Ball Control

The easiest safety to execute is one where you focus on controlling the cue ball. Because so much of the game is about cue ball control, executing a safety by sending the cue ball to an unfavorable position on the table is easiest for most players. Figure 4.16 shows a situation where you're better off playing safe on the two ball. By hitting the two thin and sending the cue ball up the table, you can create a simple safety just by controlling the cue ball.

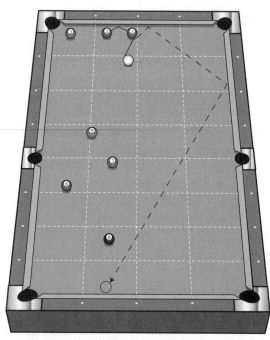

Figure 4.16 Perform this safety by controlling the cue ball.

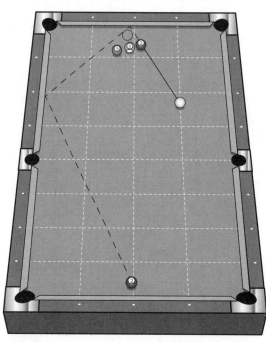

Figure 4.17 Execute this safety by controlling the object ball.

Object Ball Control

The next type of safety involves controlling the object ball. Since few players practice controlling the speed of the object ball, except to get it to the pocket, this will be a more difficult shot to master than controlling the cue ball. Nevertheless, taking time to practice object ball speed can give you a valuable tool to achieve this type of safety, especially when no other options present themselves.

Figure 4.17 illustrates a typical object ball control safety. It would be difficult in this shot to move the cue ball, but by hitting the object ball, you can send it to the other end of the table, leaving the cue ball close to the object ball's starting position. Experiment with sending object balls to parts of the table other than pockets to develop a better feel for object ball speed before trying to control these types of safe moves.

Controlling Two Balls

Not as common as the first two safety varieties, controlling both the object ball and the cue ball requires careful attention to detail. It shouldn't be as tough as players make it, since on every shot they shoot, they're sending the object ball to a pocket and the cue ball to a more advantageous spot on the table. But again, without proper knowledge of object ball speed, this shot can get tricky.

In figure 4.18, the shot presented offers one instance where controlling both balls to accomplish the safety is your best shot. As you'll note from the diagram, even if one of the balls—cue ball or object ball—doesn't quite make its mark, you've still left a very difficult shot for your opponent.

Two-Way Shots

The two-way shot—sometimes called a *free shot*—allows you to play a tough, low-percentage shot, knowing that if you miss the shot, you've still left your opponent safe. In figure 4.19, the shot on the two ball would be very difficult, made even more so by the fact that your next shot is on the three ball. The obvious choice is to opt for a safety, but wait! By attempting the bank shot shown instead, you have a chance of making the two and getting back on the three ball. Best of all, should you miss, whether by overcutting or undercutting the object ball, you've still accomplished an excellent safety.

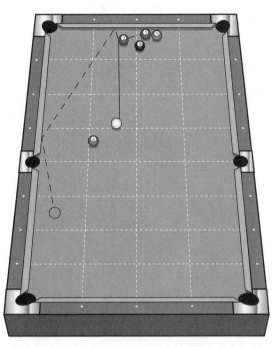

Figure 4.18 Both the object ball and the cue ball must be controlled to execute this safety.

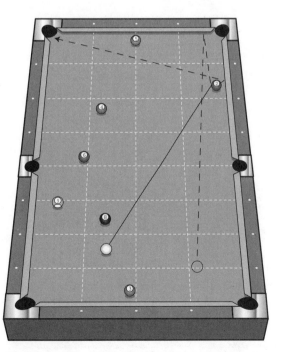

Figure 4.19 Example of a two-way shot using a bank shot. If you miss, it's okay.

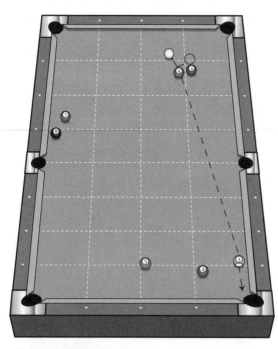

Figure 4.20 Combination shots also make for ideal two-way shot situations.

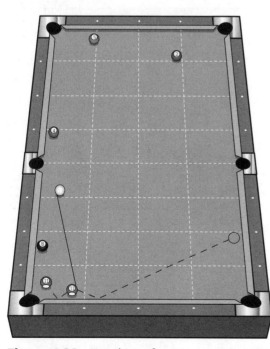

Figure 4.21 Use this safety to create a more difficult table layout for your opponent.

The other most common two-way shot is a combination shot. Figure 4.20 shows a 9-Ball game situation where the four ball can't be made, but it can be sent into the nine ball for a game win! Even if you don't pocket the nine, you can stop the cue ball, parking it neatly next to the six ball so the incoming player won't have a shot on the four.

Making a Mess

Sometimes your best safety option will be to send the object ball to a place where your opponent will be faced with a difficult run-out. You can send the object ball into another group of balls, creating clumps and clusters, or even near another ball, forcing your opponent to play a tough combination or return the safe. Another great way to make a mess of the table is to send the object ball to a spot just in front of another ball that's in line to a pocket. For example, in figure 4.21, the eight ball safety demonstrated places one of your own striped balls directly in front of the eight, between it and the pocket. The incoming player may be able to make the other solid balls but won't have a pocket for the eight ball. This increases your chances of getting back to the table.

Sometimes no shot is available at all, and an intentional

foul (tying up balls on the table) is the best "safety" even though the opponent gets ball-in-hand. This is often a better option than attempting a low-percentage kick shot, which would still give your opponent ball-in-hand but would not give you the advantage of being able to make a mess of the table.

Safety Tricks

Beyond the straightforward safety types we've just examined lie extensive tips and tricks for safeties. Safe shots, unlike your garden-variety normal shots, open up an entire world of creativity, limited only by your imagination.

Shrink the Object Ball

In any sport, the smaller the target, the tougher it is to hit. While you can't physically change the size of the balls themselves, you can make the target smaller, simply by where you leave the ball on the table. Sending the object

ball to a place near the middle of the table, or at least several inches off any cushion, makes the ball more difficult to hit with a kick shot. This is because (a) it's much easier to judge a kick when your target ball is closer to the cushion, and (b) there's more room for error. Refer to figure 4.22. In shot A, the safety left the object ball close to the rail, leaving the incoming player with several places to kick toward and still make contact on the object ball, with at least a 12-inch margin for error. But in shot B, the three ball has been left a greater distance from the rail. Now, kicking rail first, the opponent will need a highly accurate shot to get a good hit at a 2 1/4 inch target.

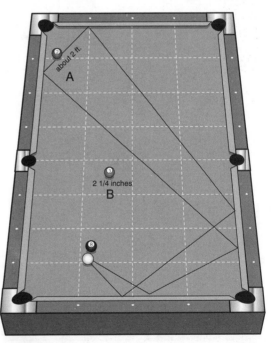

Figure 4.22 Leaving the opponent's target ball in the midst of a sea of green felt can be the best safety option.

Get Against the Wall

While your object ball is better off out in the middle of the table somewhere, your cue ball is best left as close to any cushion as possible. This immediately reduces the options for your opponent by taking away any below center shot selections. Any hit on the cue ball above center is harder to control.

Block the View

The more balls you can put between your cue ball and the object ball, the more trouble your opponent will have getting to a target. You won't always have enough balls on the table to make this scenario possible, but at the beginning of the game, especially when balls are tied up and a run-out isn't imminent, hiding the cue ball behind a wall of balls will give your opponent plenty of headaches.

Leave 'Em Long

When in doubt, leave 'em long. This slick trick is obvious but often overlooked. It's incredibly helpful in tough end game situations where there are few, if any, other object balls on the table to run interference between the cue ball and object ball. Leaving a player with a great deal of distance between balls (optimally with no easy shot to a pocket) is usually a better option than taking a low-percentage shot. Safety play, again, is about letting the other player make the mistakes.

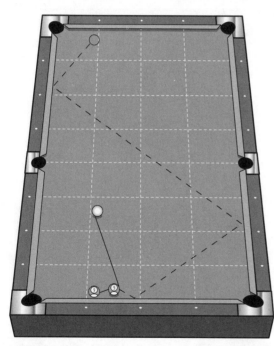

To illustrate this, we've chosen a shot you're bound to see come up time and again in match play between the pros. Figure 4.23 shows a shot you've been left on the nine ball, not very pretty at all. Rather than taking a chance on a tough bank, you can hit the nine as thinly as possible, sending the cue ball back down the table to rest on the opposite short rail, and just nudging the nine slightly closer to the other short rail. The incoming player is forced to try to return the safe or attempt a difficult, low-percentage bank shot.

Figure 4.23 Leaving a long, thin shot on the nine ball will force your opponent to attempt a tough safety or a low-percentage bank shot.

Get a Kick Out of Safes

Kick safeties are incredibly fun shots. Few players use them, though opportunities to do so come up frequently. If you become proficient at kicking balls, a kick safe isn't just effective, it's impressive! To execute kick safeties most

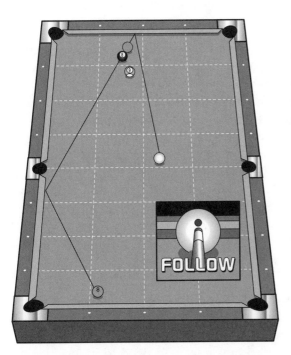

Figure 4.24 Kicking safe is an often over-looked safety option.

effectively, you first need to know how to "kill" or stop the cue ball on or near the cushion after contact with the object ball. In figure 4.24, observe the shallow-angle kick safety. When kicking at a shallow angle, you'll need to hit the cue ball with follow, which will reverse as the cue ball comes off the rail, enabling it to stop on contact with the object ball. But when the angle is wider, such as the shot shown in figure 4.25, you'll need to hit the cue ball low to stop it. A follow stroke would send it off after the object ball, while low ball actually helps "trap" the cue ball between the object ball you've just hit and the cushion.

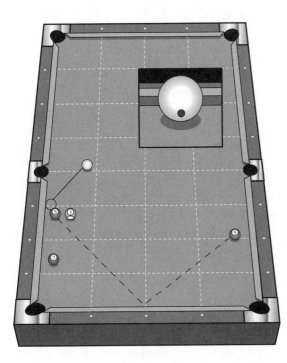

Figure 4.25 Another kick safety. Hit the cue ball low to stop this one.

Plan Ahead

Just because you have a clear shot at your next ball doesn't mean a safety won't be necessary. If the rack doesn't look promising for a run-out, you'll want to play safe, or better yet, plan ahead for a perfect safe. For instance, you may be playing 8-Ball and have a couple of open shots, but everything else is bunched up together. Play toward the bunch with your open shots; then bury your opponent with a well-executed safe. Playing 9-Ball, your strategy is usually even easier. If you have clear shots on the first several balls but know you'll be in trouble by the six ball, look for the next shot on the table that will allow you to play a game-saving safety. The more you play, the more you'll recognize when you're better off playing safe. At the same time, you'll begin to recognize more safety opportunities.

RETURNING THE JIBE

With today's prevalent one-foul, ball-in-hand rules, the best players have got to be able to shoot back at a safety played on them. When the target ball is hidden from view, this usually requires kicking rail first into the object ball. And, for obvious reasons, a player's knowledge will need to go beyond the common one-rail kick. One (or even two) rail kicks are often blocked by balls. The solution is to know several different kicking systems that will allow you to execute accurate multiple-rail kicks. Learning these systems, and the resulting tracks the cue ball will take around the table, will help you improve your safety return strategies.

One-Rail Kicks

Our first one-rail kick system works for many cross-table kicks and is easy to remember once you get the hang of it. The shot shown in figure 4.26 is an attempt to kick the one ball into the corner pocket. The first thing you need to do is determine the spot on the short rail (target rail) where the cue ball needs to make contact to successfully make the shot. In order to make this shot, you want to hit the target rail at the third diamond. Now you just have to follow the numbering convention to give this spot a value.

Starting at the far corner pocket, count the pocket as zero, the first half-diamond on the short rail as 1.0, the first diamond as 2.0, the midpoint between the first and second diamond as 2.5, the second diamond as 3.0, the midpoint between the second and third diamond as 3.5, the third diamond as 4.0, the midpoint between the third diamond and the near corner pocket as 4.5, and (finally) the corner pocket as 5.0. Note the point of contact for the shot at 4.0.

Next, you establish the relationship of the cue ball to the target area. To do this, you assign values to each half-diamond coming out of the corner pocket (closest to the one ball) along the rail where the cue ball lies (the near rail). Give that corner a value of zero and count 1.0 for each half-diamond as shown in the figure. The cue ball rests seven half-diamonds away from the corner pocket.

Now you do the math. Remember in the first step we said that you're looking to hit the third diamond as your final destination? And you assigned a value of 4.0 to that destination? Count 4.0 for each half-diamond out of the corner pocket as determined in the last step. If the cue ball rests at the near rail, seven half-diamonds out of the right corner pocket, that's equal to 28 (4.0 × 7 half-diamonds). Okay, put your pocket calculator away. The math is over!

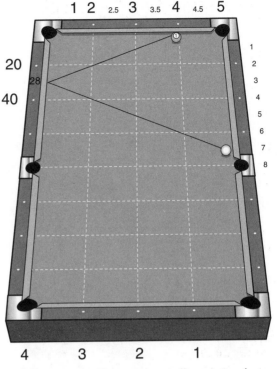

Figure 4.26 The numbers allow a simple one-rail kicking system.

Next, all you do is find the value 28 on the far rail. The right corner pocket along that rail is assigned zero, and each diamond is assigned a value in increments of 20 (the first diamond is 20, the second is 40). The 28 spot is about two fifths of the way up from the first diamond to the second. It may be useful to think in half-diamonds of 10 points each, so the 28 spot is just short of the halfway point between the second and third half-diamonds. Another way to think about the far rail is that it has a value of 10 times the value you assigned to the near rail. So, the target would be directly across from 2.8 on the near rail. Be careful when your target is between the corner pocket and the first half-diamond, because you may have a tendency to place the starting (zero) point deep in the pocket. Ensure that your distances are equal by starting your measurements at the end of the pocket flange, or in line with the bottom rail bumper.

Notice that if you move the cue ball to the right three half-diamonds (to 4), your target on the far rail becomes 16 (4.0 × 4), roughly three quarters the distance from the pocket to the first diamond. Similarly, if the spot on the target rail (the object ball) moves to the corner pocket, the half-diamond value changes to 5.0, and the far rail target becomes 35 (5.0 × 7 half-diamonds).

It's very important to hit this shot with medium speed and no english. Any spin on the cue ball will change the angle from its intended path. A shot hit too hard will compress the rail and spit the cue ball back out, sending it short of the target. Be sure to begin the numbering system from the corner pocket on the far rail.

Figure 4.27 demonstrates a system useful in one-rail, length-of-the-table kicking. The cue ball is on the short rail, and you need to hit a ball on the long rail to your right. In the example, you are trying to contact the five ball that's hanging in the side pocket. To determine the spot on the opposite short rail to hit first, you'll assign it numbers.

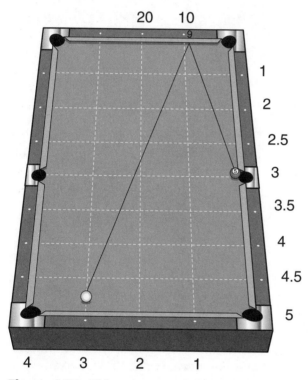

Figure 4.27 This system is useful for learning one-rail kicks the length of the table.

Since the ball you want to hit is on your right as you face the rail you're aiming toward, everything starts on the right. For the near short rail, start with the first diamond on your right and number the diamonds (1, 2, 3, and 4) as in the diagram. (Note that 4 is actually the corner pocket on your left.)

Next, you assign numbers on the opposite short rail. Here, you need only assign numbers to the center diamond and the diamond between the center and the corner pocket on your right, because you are kicking on the right half of the table. Number them 10 and 20 as shown. (One way to remember this is that these values are 10 times the value of their near short rail counterpart. That is, when you move in a straight line across from the number 2 diamond on your near short rail to your far short rail, that diamond value is 20, or 2 × 10).

Okay, last set of numbering instructions—the long rail. Start at the far end of the table and work your way to the corner pocket nearest you. As noted on the diagram, number the diamonds as follows: 1, 2, 2.5, 3 (side pocket), 3.5, 4, 4.5, 5 (corner pocket).

Time to assess the situation. The cue ball is on the number 3 diamond on the near short rail, and you want to move it to the 3.0 diamond on the long rail. To do so, simply multiply 3 × 3. You have now mastered this one-rail kick system. All you need to do now is find the 9 spot on the far short rail—just right of the first diamond.

There are a couple things to remember with this system. First, for the cue ball to run its truest course, use just a touch of follow with no sidespin. Any sidespin will throw off the angle of deflection that you calculated, altering the path of the cue ball and the subsequent outcome of the shot. Next, keep in mind that the target on the long rail is the point on the line *between* the diamonds, not necessarily the point in *front* of the diamond you are trying to hit. So aim *through* the diamond, not at the spot on the rail in front of it. Similarly, the cue ball must be on the track between the numbered diamonds (between 1 and 4 on the near rail) for this system to work without adjustments. Any time the cue ball is not on the track, it gets more difficult and becomes an art of minor adjustment. (You can still use the system as a guide in these situations.) If the ball you want to kick is on the left side of the table, say in the other side pocket, you will need to reverse the numbering system so that everything starts on the left. That's all there is to it!

Here's a system for a one-rail kick that comes up all the time. Figure 4.28 indicates how to find the spot on the rail to hit and kick an object ball in the corner when another object ball is blocking a direct shot. First, find the contact point on the object ball. Note the distance between this point and the

rail. Then double that distance back from the rail as shown. (It's easiest if you use your cue tip or finger to measure this distance.) Next, drop your line of aim from that point to the cue ball. Where the line crosses the rail is where you will aim the cue ball. This allows you to visualize an equilateral triangle, where one of the equal sides is the path the cue ball will take when it rebounds from the rail, using the "angle in equals angle out" principle. Practice this shot with the object ball only an inch or so off the rail before slowly increasing the distance from the rail. When the angle is sharper, use a touch of running english to "open" the angle.

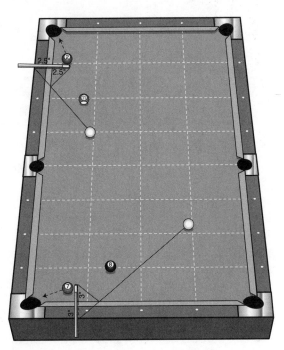

Figure 4.28 Using your cue stick to measure kicking distance.

Spin

As you've already learned, spin will always be a factor in shot selection, and kicks are no exception. The following illustrations will help you plan your path. Figure 4.29 demonstrates the effects that spin has on the angle of deflection off the first rail. The center ball hit, demonstrated by the cue ball in the lowest position on the table, takes an "angle in equals angle out" path. The cue ball starts at a point six diamonds from the corner pocket. By dividing this by two you find your center ball hit on the opposite rail to go into the corner. Hit this shot with medium speed.

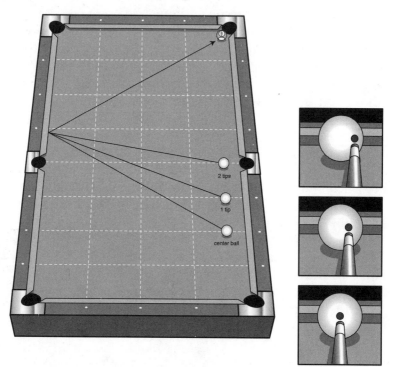

Figure 4.29 Changing the kicking angle with spin off the cushion.

Moving one diamond closer to the pocket will put the cue ball five diamonds from the corner pocket. By using one tip of right english, you can still hit the third diamond on the other side of the table and make the nine ball. When you move the cue ball up yet another diamond toward the side pocket, you must apply two tips of right english to achieve the same result. Experiment with these examples to gauge how much spin your stroke will put on the ball. Adjust your speed until you achieve the best results.

Figure 4.30 demonstrates the effect of inside or reverse english applied to the cue ball off the first rail. Find the angle in/angle out hit to make the one ball by splitting the difference in distance between the cue ball and the one ball. Now, if you move the cue ball to the third diamond along the long rail and use one tip of left english, you'll still be able to pocket the one ball by hit-

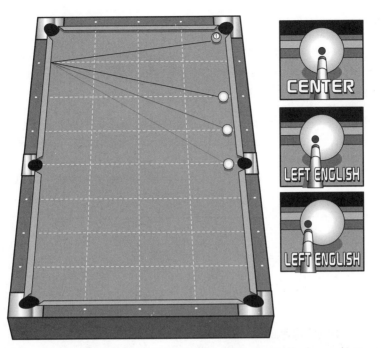

Figure 4.30 Using inside (reverse) english to kick in a ball, dependent on the cue ball's position on the rail.

ting the first diamond from the corner on the opposite side of the table. You can move down another diamond toward the side pocket, use two tips of left english, and still make the one ball in the corner. Remember, when using inside english, you must hit the cue ball firmer to keep that spin on the cue ball, forcing it to react as planned.

Figure 4.31 illustrates how to deviate from the natural deflection of the cue ball using extreme spin. This shot uses a medium hit with two tips of left english. This spins the cue ball, which is hit directly into the center diamond on the short rail, back to the side pocket where it neatly pockets the nine.

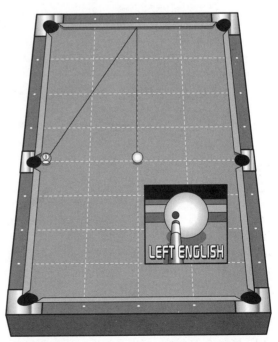

Figure 4.31 Using extreme left english, you can shoot directly at the center diamond on the short rail, as shown, to pocket the ball in the side.

Another shot that comes in handy when the natural track is blocked is shown in figure 4.32. With the cue ball in front of the left corner pocket, hit the first diamond on the far short rail with two tips of right (running) english to make the one ball in the opposite corner. Similarly, aim at the third diamond with two tips of left (reverse) english to hold the angle and kick the two ball in the same corner pocket. Here again, invest the time to experiment with your stroke and speed on these shots. Once you know where your stroke and speed will take your cue ball, using inside or outside spin will be an asset.

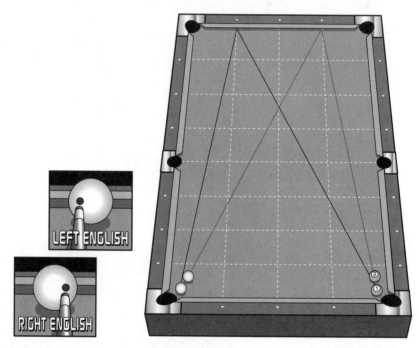

Figure 4.32 Experiment with this shot using both left and right english to know the variety of hits you can execute to still pocket this kick.

The Poison Path

Scratching in the side pocket is an all-too-familiar scenario, but it never becomes any less frustrating! In order to keep the cue ball on the table where it belongs, you must be able to recognize the "poison path" and steer clear of danger. Figure 4.33 shows three roads to destruction as the cue ball comes out from the corner of the table. Once you recognize that track, here's a little trick to help. Pick out a spot on the wall (roughly nine feet away) that runs past the table from that track. Any time your cue ball is rolling toward the spot you've picked, you'll know to watch out. As time goes on you'll simply be aware of these tracks on the table and avoid them. The best way to avoid scratching in the side is to adjust your angle either by going a diamond long or a diamond short of the side pocket.

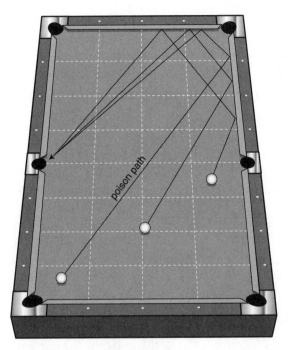

Figure 4.33 Tracks give us direction, keeping us from scratching in the side pockets.

Two-Rail Kicks

When the one-rail track is blocked, this two-rail system is very handy and easy to see. Figure 4.34 demonstrates two shots using this system, one shot sending the three ball toward the right side pocket, and the other shot sending the four ball toward the upper left corner pocket. To determine the point on the first rail to hit, draw an imaginary line between the cue ball and the object ball and find its center point. Drop a perpendicular line from that point to the center of the pocket you are going to shoot around. Then find the parallel line that runs through the cue ball to the first rail to find your target. Shoot at that spot with a center ball, medium hit.

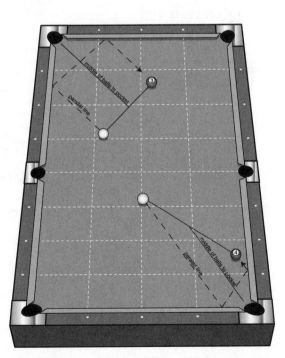

Figure 4.34 Two examples of two-rail kicks.

Once you have found your starting point on the first rail, you can further refine what you wish to do with the shot. If your intention is to drive the ball being kicked a great distance, you'll want to get a full hit on the ball at a greater speed. But if you increase your speed, you'll shorten the angle off the cushions, so you'll need to adjust accordingly.

Three-Rail Kicks

Sometimes the one-rail and even the two-rail tracks are blocked from your use, and it becomes necessary to look for other options. Here is a three-rail kick option that will help when that happens. Figure 4.35 demonstrates tracks that will all roughly lead to diamond 2 on the third rail, which in turn will bring the cue ball to the lower left corner pocket.

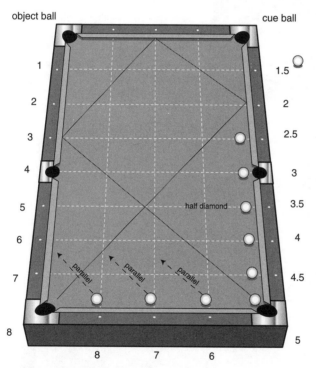

Figure 4.35 This three-rail kicking system can be a lifesaver in trouble spots.

To begin, as always, you need a numbering convention. Start the numbering on the first rail at the corner pocket farthest from the cue ball (upper left) as follows: 0, 1, 2, 3, 4 (side pocket), 5, 6, 7, 8 (corner pocket, aka the target). Now for the near rail numbers start with the upper right corner pocket: 0, 1.5, 2, 2.5, 3 (right side pocket), 3.5, 4, 4.5. Then continue that numbering along the near rail in *whole* numbers: 5 (right lower corner pocket), 6, 7, 8.

Now let's find the tracks. To do this, remember that the third rail target is the number 2 diamond. If the cue ball is positioned at the number 7 diamond on the near rail, then the first rail target is 5 (7 − 2). Similarly, if the cue ball is positioned on the number 8 diamond, the first rail target is 6 (8 − 2). Notice that these tracks create parallel lines all across the table.

However, this only holds through to the 3 − 2 track. Once the cue ball moves above this track, your diamond increments are cut in half. Notice that if the cue ball is at the first diamond up on the right (4.5), the target on the first rail becomes 2.5 (4.5 − 2). This line is not parallel to the other tracks. This is because when coming off the first rail into the second rail, the angle shortens up, and when the cue ball moves toward the third rail it opens up again.

If the cue ball is not directly on a track, find the closest track and drop a parallel line to it. Aim *through* the diamond, not at the spot on the rail in front of it. Remember that the speed of the shot will affect the rebound angles. When hitting harder than normal, aim longer or wider on the first rail.

As you can see, mapping the table involves plenty of knowledge, paired with careful strategy and pure creativity. Simply put, the more you know about your table mapping options, including the variety of tracks the cue ball can take around the bed of the pool table, the more options you'll have available to execute the sharpest offensive and defensive moves.

5

Mastering the Mind Game

What separates the great players from average recreational players isn't necessarily raw talent, or even having the most knowledge. It's *applied* knowledge—knowing how to use your talent and acquired skills to the best advantage, how to make the most of your practice time, how to exercise physical and mental discipline at the table, how to develop and maintain confidence in your skills, and most of all, how to enjoy your victories and learn from your defeats.

PRACTICE MAKES PERFECT

You've probably heard the worn cliche since you were a kid, but without question, if you want to accelerate your pool progress, then practice is required. On the physical side of the sport, regular practice is what helps you build muscle memory, allowing your body to stand, bend, and execute shots with minimum effort and maximum efficiency. If you've ever had to take time off from your pool game, you'll recall that all the things that came as naturally as riding a bike, from sighting a shot to following through, weren't as automatic when you resumed playing. Regular practice offers you the benefit of smooth, effortless motion, unhampered by thoughts of what must be done at each stage of the game (thoughts which break up the physical action).

A good example is your pre-shot routine. If you've practiced it enough to make it an automatic response to approaching each shot, you'll realize that it has become a linked chain of events that occur naturally as you play. But if you don't practice your pre-shot routine and make it part of your game, you'll approach some shots with a full routine and others struggling to remember all the elements you should be managing. Throughout this chapter, watch for some easy and fun drills to keep your practice sessions fresh and interesting.

As all players know, pool is as much a mental game as a physical sport. In the past few chapters, you've seen how much there is to learn and remember about the game, from types of shot selections, to types of pattern plays, to safeties and kicking systems. Reading this book without applying the knowledge in regular practice sessions won't do much to build your mental game, and knowing how to pocket a ball without a clue as to where to go next will quickly diminish your interest in the sport.

How to Practice

Some players prefer to practice with a partner; others prefer to play alone. Frankly, it's important to do both. Playing with a partner offers situations you tend not to see when playing alone. Playing solo allows you to focus on target areas of your game that need work.

No matter where, when, or with whom you practice, it's how you practice that counts. When you practice, have a purpose in mind. Take a moment to self-analyze your game. If you're weak on cue ball control, focus on pinpoint position, or try to get the cue ball to the center of the table after each shot. If you can't seem to play a decent safety, throw out a rack of balls and try to play safe on each one, then try to kick your way out of your own safeties.

DISCIPLINE AT THE TABLE

Naturally, you're not learning all the amazing things you can learn about pool just to spend your days practicing. The learning and the practice are preparation for the ultimate in pool—the competition. Sure, all players have different competitive goals, from beating their best friend, to besting the other teams in their local bar league, to winning an amateur tournament, to cracking the professional ranks. But no matter the goals they set, or where they want to take their pool talents, they will all have certain things in common, and one of them is how they conduct themselves—physically, mentally, and psychologically—at the table.

Physical Success

Let's face it, if you're a physical mess, this will eventually translate to your skills at the table. Again, using the professionals as the benchmark for physical discipline, let's peek into the pro ranks to observe their tactics for enhanced physical performance.

Pool is like any other sport. If you don't feel good, you won't perform well. Serious professionals maintain a decent regimen that includes getting enough sleep before a key match, working out (long matches demand much more endurance than one might expect from a nonaerobic sport), dressing comfortably (tight or ill-fitting clothing doesn't go well with bending and stretching

How the Pros Practice

Even professionals are sometimes challenged by how to incorporate quality practice ideas into their daily regimens. We polled dozens of pros to pull together their favorite practice tips; then we evaluated the effectiveness of each suggestion as it might relate to your own practice routine.

I spend most of my time working on the break, as it's a critical shot in 9-Ball today.

The break is definitely a critical shot in today's 9-Ball competition. But you have to keep in mind that at the professional level, the more rudimentary aspects of the game have long since become second nature, so more time can be invested on specific shots like this. Spend 10 minutes of your practice time on the break—you'll increase your ability and your confidence in this shot without sacrificing other aspects of your game.

I just keep breaking racks and attempting to run them out.

This offers a more well-rounded practice routine. Your break gets plenty of practice, as does your offensive game. You can work on pattern plays, cue ball control, and aggressive offense. When you get out of line, you'll be tempted to try critical shots like curves and banks, which hone your offensive game. On the flip side, you won't spend much time on your defensive game, and you'll usually go for shots that are familiar to you, rather than experimenting or practicing shots you don't yet have firmly in your arsenal.

I work on precise position play drills, like getting the cue ball back to the center of the table after each shot.

We love the cue ball to the center of the table drill, and it's definitely important to work on precise position play. But drills can get tedious, even to the most disciplined player. Mix it up by running a few racks, then working a drill, and then going back to a break and run.

I work on speed control by picking an exact spot on the table for every shot I'm shooting, and then trying to get the cue ball there. If I don't, I have to shoot it again until I do.

This is an excellent routine to incorporate into your practice. It forces you to demand the most from each shot you shoot. Unlike attempting to run a rack, where you may miss and just keep shooting, you'll have to shoot the shot again and again until you get it perfect. This increases your confidence, along with building mind and muscle memory for every shot you encounter in your practice session. In addition, you can use this routine just as easily with safety opportunities you come upon. Work each shot as its own piece of art, and you'll soon build a tremendous data bank of perfect plays.

(continued)

(continued)

I work on safeties by trying to snooker myself on every shot and then trying to kick my way out of the safe.

A perfect part of every practice session, but make sure you practice offense too. You need to spend just as much time pocketing balls so that you'll have the talent and confidence to play your offensive game.

I practice banks, shooting off the rail, and shooting with my bridge hand jacked up over balls to make sure I have confidence in the tougher situations I'm bound to be faced with.

It's true, those top-shelf shots we showed you earlier are certainly an integral part of any professional's game, and they'll help yours too. Nevertheless, investing too much of your practice time on these, like any one segment of your game, will not make you a well-rounded player. Like practicing breaks (as described for the first player response), it works for players who have mastered other key elements of the game, but not for most players.

What you can learn from the responses offered so far is that different players consider different elements of the sport as the key to their success: breaking, offensive play, cue ball control, safeties, and top-shelf shots.

I try to play by myself and only play with partners who are better players than me.

This practice suggestion isn't always practical, is it? While we heartily agree that solo practice is necessary to learn plenty of skills and strategies, playing with someone better isn't always an option. Imagine how difficult this must be for the pros.

It's true, playing with players who are better than you will teach you plenty about the game, every time you play. But what about them? No matter whom you play—better or worse, faster or slower, amateur or pro—you can learn just as much about your own game.

Further, if you become used to playing competitors of all skill levels, you'll learn one of the most important mental advantages in the sport—it's usually smarter to play the table, not the other player. As you'll soon read, there are exceptions to every rule, but for now, focus on your game, no matter who you play.

for shots), and eating properly (there's nothing worse than running out of gas midway through a match).

This is all commonsense stuff, but again, because pool is a nonaerobic, nonreactive, and noncontact sport, aspiring players often ignore the physical aspect, thinking they can make up for it with their mental game. Unfortunately, if their body isn't working, even players with plenty of confidence will begin to suffer as their game heads south. And, the more popular and lucrative the sport becomes, with bigger purses, sponsors, and televised tours, the more athletic types will be drawn to play. That steps the competition up a notch, forcing players who haven't been in good shape to get there, and fast!

One way plenty of pro players (both male and female) stay in shape and get away from pool is playing golf. These sports are similar in many respects, and golf offers players the chance to get a bit of fresh air and plenty of walking. Stretching exercises are also excellent for the pool player, along with swimming and yoga. These types of activities offer improved muscle tone yet allow the flexibility in the muscles needed to execute shots (a flexible wrist is always a plus for making the cue ball dance). These activities help keep leg, back, shoulder, and neck muscles flexible and toned; these are the areas hardest hit by continual standing, bending, and reaching for shots.

Once you arrive at your match, there's a new cache of physical tactics available to enhance your performance. First and most obvious, you must relax. The more important the match at hand, the more difficult it will be to do this. But if you can't relax, your muscles will tighten up, and you won't be able to feel your swing. The best two physical methods of relaxation are to (a) breathe and (b) consciously relax your muscles, one by one, beginning with dropping your neck and shoulders.

As the match progresses, you'll be spending some time in your chair while your opponent is at the table. It's one of those unchangeable facts of pool—get used to it. But, if you have something to do while you're grounded there waiting for your turn, you'll be ready to approach the table again, and you'll keep your mind and body from losing their focus. One way to keep your physical attention on the game is to focus firmly on the cue ball. Physically, this allows you to continue looking at the table (not around the room or at your opponent or at the good-looking player across the way) and will offer you plenty of insights—how fast or slow the cloth is playing, reaction of the cushions, and so forth. You'll know immediately if your opponent misses or commits a foul, and you'll be ready to step up for your next shot. This is also an excellent mental trick to keep you "in the game" and keep your mind from wandering.

The other practices you need to keep up while in your chair are your muscle relaxation and relaxed breathing. It won't help to begin the match relaxed if you become tense while your opponent is at the table. All players are susceptible to this, especially if their opponent is spending a great deal of time at the table, running out. But, if you tense up in your chair, and your opponent suddenly misses, chances are you will jump to the table unready to play. This happens even in the pro ranks. Sometimes a player misses a shot unexpectedly, leaving an easy shot for the opponent, who approaches the table eagerly (but not prepared) and misses right back. It's a senseless way to give up a game. But it's easily prevented by realizing that even when you're not playing, you have to remain in the game!

Mental Success

The biggest mistake *all* players make is not having a clear mental picture of what they're doing, and where they're going, on every shot. You can't be involved in the sport for long without hearing these famous last words, "I couldn't make up my mind on that shot," or "My cue ball ended up right between the two places I was trying to decide on." Whenever they cannot immediately see the next shot, most players take a walk around the table. Sometimes changing your perspective allows you to see a shot you otherwise would overlook.

Professional player Vivian Villarreal mentally prepares before attempting her shot.

Surprise, surprise. Your body can only do what your mind tells it to do! If your mind isn't made up, it's basically telling your body to compromise. So you won't get to the place you intended, and you will usually end up with a bad combination of the options you were considering. Once you pick an option, commit to it, and your body can only follow.

Another key mental problem is not examining your options in the first place. You're so happy to get back to the table with an easy shot that you jump down and cinch the ball, only to find you're going to be in deep trouble a couple balls later. Your pre-shot routine must include examining your available options on each and every shot. For example, a good shot may indeed be lying there waiting for you, but if you haven't said to yourself, "Self, am I better off playing a safety here?" *before* deciding which option to exercise, you're only playing half your game.

On the flip side of this coin, overthinking can be just as damaging to your mental game. Unfortunately, pool is an easy sport to overthink. The more you know, the more you can fall into this trap. Say, for example, you have quite a command of critical shots, and you are presented with a difficult bank, a thin cut, or a safety option. You may veer toward the option of shooting the critical shot simply because you know it, when in fact the safety is your best bet. This is where three very important phrases come into play:

1. Keep it simple, Stupid! (KISS)
2. Play the percentages.
3. Take the path of least resistance.

It's true that the shot you are faced with may present a dozen options to your well-educated brain, but it's easy to eliminate most with these three phrases. Pick the easiest, keep it simple, and execute the shot with the best percentage for success.

Finally, it helps to recognize what's probable versus what's possible. There is a tendency, when players try to get a bit too creative, to try something that may indeed be possible according to universal law but sure isn't probable. Such attempts are usually accompanied by a cry of "What was I thinking?" and are easy to avoid if you pay attention.

In addition, your physical and mental skills at the table will be equally enhanced by closely observing what is happening on the playing surface. Incorporate what you observe into your mind's ever-burgeoning data bank of pool knowledge. Here are several things to look for:

1. **What's the best shot on the table?** What would you do if it were your shot? After a quick survey of the table, determine the strategy you would take, then see what the shooter does. Did the shooter's plan match yours? Did the plan conclude satisfactorily or did it go awry? Could anything have been done to change the outcome? By remembering the concept of the shot, you will be able to recognize a similar situation in the future and avoid its pitfalls.

2. **Why did the shooter do that?** Sometimes your opponent will do something that you don't understand. Sometimes he has a plan in mind that hasn't occurred to you. There is an advantage and a disadvantage to every shot. By observing, for example, a situation where your opponent played a good safe when you would have opted for a bank, you can learn more about the risk and reward factors in your own game.

3. **Observe everyone.** It's just as important to witness unsuccessful strategies as it is to witness successful executions. A shot can be learned from any player, from the beginner to the seasoned professional. While you may assume that you will learn the most from seasoned players, the fact is that many beginners have a unique approach they've invented without the encumbrance of too much instruction, and that approach may just work for you!

4. **What are your opponent's strengths and weaknesses?** The best strategists know the strengths and weaknesses of their opponent. The only way to learn them is to observe. In addition, when you observe an opponent objectively, you achieve a level of detachment that keeps the game analytical, rather than succumbing to emotional and psychological responses.

Psychological Success

You're thinking right. You're playing well. You're paying attention. Can you still fall apart at the table? Sadly, yes. Even if your physical and mental skills are right on target, there will be those times when you give away a match for seemingly no good reason. Rather than forcing your opponent to defeat you with her skills, you lose because, in simple terms, you beat yourself.

This is where the psychology of pool comes into play. Your attitude can beef up your physical and mental skills, or destroy them. But the attitude problems usually fall into one of a few categories. Knowing the following list of tongue-in-cheek psychological syndromes as they apply to pool might help. Note: These are not medical terms, but rather a collection of psychological problems players have expressed to us over the years.

1. **The work/fun syndrome.** This one will rear its ugly head in one of two ways. First, there's the player who isn't having any fun, laboring over each shot with a do-or-die attitude that's painful to observe. These players put so much pressure on themselves that you wonder if they won't crack right in half with one more miss. Unfortunately, misses are imminent, since the body simply cannot relax and do its job when so much pressure is being put on it to perform. These players will also be likely to quickly tire out in a match, because the energy that must be sustained is great when under that much pressure.

Conversely, the other type of player exhibiting this syndrome believes that since this is a game, and it should be fun, no thinking whatsoever should be required. And that's perfectly okay for the recreational player. But for those aspiring to higher levels of play, we submit that the thinking part can be fun, too. The joy of pool lies not only in banging balls around the table, but also in challenging yourself to play complex patterns and think your way out of tough situations. Since pool combines the physical talents required of other sports like golf and archery, and the mental acuities of thinking games like chess, labyrinths, and brainteasers, you have the ideal atmosphere to have fun while still taking your game seriously.

2. **The whiner syndrome.** Also referred to as the "poor me" syndrome, this one causes players to find fault in everything—the bad luck of the draw, the way the table is playing, bad rolls, and every other complaint you can imagine. Players with whiner syndrome are easy to spot, even if they're whining to themselves, because they typically exhibit this syndrome in their body language, too. If you've ever come upon opponents who trudge to the table, sigh often, and look like they're wearing an invisible 100-pound vest on their slumping shoulders, you know the type. You'll also probably know that they're easy to beat—hide the cue ball a few times and they'll swear they get more bad rolls than anyone else in life. Jump ahead a game or two and they'll fold like a cheap suit.

3. **The opponent barometer syndrome.** Like the work/fun syndrome, this one can manifest itself in two ways. First, let's say you've drawn a tough

player. There is a strong psychological tendency to play the player and not the table. You go into the match an underdog, and you lose out of respect for the unspoken pecking order. But let's face it, if this were true, the top-ranked players would *always* be the top-ranked players. They get beat because others believe in themselves enough to know they have a chance to win, too.

Second, there are players you may underestimate, which is equally dangerous. When you underestimate opponents, no matter their skill level, you give them opportunities you wouldn't dare give better players. You take risks you normally wouldn't take. In pool, this is often referred to as playing like you will get another chance at the table, or "letting up" on your opponent. You expect that even if you miss, so what, the other player can't possibly run out. It's safe to say more "upsets" occur in tournaments because of underestimating opponents than overestimating them.

4. **The "I'm not worthy" syndrome.** Similar to overestimating an opponent, "I'm not worthy" players give their opponents unnecessary gifts out of a sense of fair play. Let's say, for example, you know you haven't practiced at all for the tournament in which you're about to play, and you're suddenly facing a player whom you're quite capable of beating. But, you give the match away with stupid mistakes because your subconscious is telling you that you don't deserve to win—your opponent has worked harder for it. Or, say you get a series of really good rolls on the table (and it happens as often as the bad ones, make no mistake!) and again, you let up on your game—and your opponent—out of guilt. Yet another example involves the financial aspect of cash tournaments, where you might be sitting pretty but feeling bad for your opponent who scraped up his last $5 or $500 to participate.

Every aspect of this syndrome suggests that you're perhaps taking the sport too seriously. Remember the old adage, "It's just a game." Treat it as such—forget the personalities, forget the money, forget the guilt, and simply "play to play." This major attitude adjustment will bring you back to your memories of playing pool for the sheer enjoyment of the game and allow you to compete unhampered by excess baggage.

5. **The control freak syndrome.** This one happens to the best of us and refers to trying to overcontrol the table by overcontrolling your body. This can't be done. The balls are round, and they will roll, often a hair past where you needed them to be. You won't have a shot. Deal with it. Don't try to bend your will through your cue, as you'll only tighten your muscles and nerves to the breaking point. Instead, relax, breathe, and view the situation as an opportunity to challenge your wits and your creativity.

Everybody (and we mean everybody) has fallen victim to one or more of these syndromes at some point in their playing career. But if you can honestly diagnose the problem, you're halfway to solving it and once again enjoying the competition.

CONFIDENCE

Everything you do in life requires confidence, whether you're working, driving down the road, or playing in a pool tournament. Without confidence, your moves at the table will be hesitant, your brain will think negative thoughts, and you will not survive a match. When you are confident, you're more relaxed, you can't be intimidated, and you can let go of missed shots and opportunities more quickly (and proceed to what can be done to recover the game). Confidence helps you focus on the positive, maintain those positive thoughts, and trust your abilities in crucial situations.

Believe in Yourself

Confidence can be elusive for many pool players, probably because there's so much for them to learn, and so much that can go wrong, either mentally or physically, in any given game. Pool may be the toughest sport there is because so many of a player's resources are required to perform well. Nevertheless, there are steps you can take to improve your confidence:

- **Natural ability.** If you naturally see shot angles, complete table patterns, and safety opportunities, you already have a natural mental ability to play pool. Likewise, if you can jump to the table without warming up and pocket several balls in succession, chances are you have natural physical talent. There are plenty of pros who may not be the best shot makers, but they'll play an amazing defensive game, use their head, and make sure that their opponent is the one left making mistakes with low-percentage shots. Conversely, we know many professional players who may not have as much knowledge or mental strategy in their game, but they can shoot their way out of a bad situation from anywhere. Confidence in their physical abilities enables them to do so. If you're really lucky, you've got both. Your natural mental and physical ability is the first step toward confidence, but if you aren't convinced you've got much in either department, no worries, keep reading!

- **Practice.** This can't be said too often: The more you know about the game, the more confidence you'll have in your abilities. This is no different than riding a bike. It doesn't matter if you've last ridden five years ago or yesterday. Because you learned once, when you get on the bike, you'll have faith in your ability to pedal it down the street without falling over. Likewise, should you see a shot in competition that you've made countless times in practice, you will naturally have the confidence in your ability to pocket the ball and play position for your next shot. Each time you develop a new skill and add it to your toolbox through study and practice, you're building a solid foundation on which confidence can easily perch. The more you practice, the more you will find familiar when it comes time for an actual competition.

- **Experience.** Many players have a different level of confidence in competition than they do in practice. Good practice players have high confidence in practice, but they lack confidence in competition. Confidence under pressure comes from performing well under pressure. To develop confidence, you have to play up to your ability while competing and play just as good *if not better* than you do in practice. The more times you beat someone, the more you can draw from that well of confidence to use it in your next match.

• **Mental imaging.** Imagine yourself being successful. Picture in your mind's eye the entire match, resulting in your victory. Imagine everything from running racks, to moving your score up, to crisply pocketing the game ball, to shaking your opponent's hand and hearing the applause of the audience. If you can imagine a successful result to your competition, you can develop confidence in your ability to make the imagined result a reality.

Make this mental imaging part of your practice routine. Don't leave the practice table until you've imagined yourself in a winning situation. You may find that you feel a little nervous even visualizing such a match. That's good! It means you're doing an excellent job of visualizing the situation. It also means you're practicing (just by imagining) how to deal with this nervousness. By feeling the adrenaline rush in your mind, you're practicing the art of functioning under pressure, which will make real pressure situations that much easier to handle.

Remember, it's important to *maintain* your confidence too. Does one bad shot ruin your confidence? Does a tiny voice in your head haunt you with words like, "What are you *doing*?" For many pool players, confidence seems to vary from moment to moment, depending on the situation. Confidence should be based on past successes, many hours of practice, and your subsequent honed skills at the table. After all, you have "paid your dues." You deserve to be confident.

Beware of Confidence Killers

Even the top players in the world can lose their confidence despite glowing track records. There are four huge confidence killers that will try to emerge when you play, bouncing around your mind like childish, unwanted guests. Be mindful. Don't let them in when they come knocking:

1. **Excuses, excuses.** You cannot feel confident if you look for excuses why you didn't play up to your potential. Imagining success means looking for reasons to play well rather than excuses to play poorly. Expect good things to happen rather than fear what might go wrong. See yourself playing your best pool rather than visualizing mistakes and poor play.

2. **External circumstances.** Think only about what you can control at the table—your body, your mind, your decisions, and your results. Many players let external circumstances control their confidence meters. Do bad rolls affect your confidence? Do you feel intimidated when you play a seasoned player? Does crowd noise suddenly make you unable to concentrate? Don't dwell on

the circumstances that surround your game situation. Expend your energy on the things you *can* control, such as the quality of your practice time and your effort to be mentally prepared to play your best pool.

3. **Fear factors.** It's been said that, "Fear is the wrong use of imagination." It's been said that, "The only thing we have to fear is fear itself." It's been said that, "Faith and fear cannot coexist." It's high time you listened. Whether it's a tiny fear (a particular shot, for example) or a big one (fear of your opponent, fear of losing a match or tournament), it needs to be addressed and reframed in your mind's eye. Fear causes hesitation, awkward movements, and extra adrenaline that can shake up your arms and your shots.

Part of the problem with fear factors is that everyone has a few, but nobody wants to admit to them, even to themselves. It's easier to say the other guy got lucky than to admit you were afraid you couldn't measure up. Nevertheless, as taught in all those hero movies, real courage is about facing the fear, meeting it head-on, and plodding through. Pool is no different. Every fear factor you will encounter has an antidote if you're tough enough to face the fact that you've got it. Here are some common fear factors:

- **Fear of shots.** All players have shots they're not comfortable attempting, but different reactions to the fear produce different outcomes. If you "poke and hope," you may make it, and you can act indifferent if you don't make it. You can practice the shot until it doesn't evoke visions of embarrassment in your mind. You can make a mental note to practice it before the next event, but also make your best attempt to do it right this time. In the third option, you allow yourself to feel uncomfortable about the shot, but at least have faith in your ability to give it a go.

- **Fear of opponents.** What did we tell you about playing the table? If you're afraid of your opponent because she is better than you, play the table. Remember, everyone (including you!) knows your opponent is better anyway, so what have you got to lose? Ah, but if you win . . .

Many top players actually put more pressure on themselves when playing a lesser player. They already know this player has nothing to lose, and they often fear the opposite, that they'll look really silly if they get beat by someone they shouldn't. Again, play the table. Let your confidence go to work for you. You've got the game, you've got the experience, you've got the talent. Use it!

- **Fear of humiliation.** It's been said that fear would not exist without pain, whether mental or physical, and the mental is what we're talking about here. Players fear not playing their best game in front of friends, family, and fans. They fear embarrassing themselves with a poor performance or a stupid mistake. They fear recrimination from their coaches. But if they allow all these fears to cloud their focus at the table, they're toast.

The best antidote to this fear is to reframe your reason for being in the match. Are you playing for your family, friends, fans, or coach? No! You play because you enjoy playing. Keep your focus on the table, and play your game for you alone, not for anyone else. This takes the pressure off and allows you to perform to the best of *your* ability instead of allowing others to define your ability. It is, after all, only a game—keep having fun!

4. **Overconfidence.** Finally, be honest with yourself. You can act confident and develop your confidence, but having a false sense of confidence can be deadly in strategic pool. Knowing your skills (in which you may have great confidence) *and* your limitations (in which you will not) can actually increase your confidence because you'll play smarter pool. For instance, rolling out to a jump shot in a game of 9-Ball, when you haven't yet acquired the solid skills (with practice) to make this shot, is exhibiting false confidence. You are attempting a shot that you know (if you are honest with yourself) you can't make. If you fail, the other player runs out. Now your confidence in your ability to shoot and win has eroded. Even if you make it, you'll be feeling a little guilty, knowing you got away with it but didn't necessarily deserve it. And the thought will nag at your brain, chipping away at your focus. Instead, play those percentages. If you're more confident in the bank shot than the safety, by all means, go for it. But if you know it's a low-percentage shot for you, have the confidence in your mental game to think of a better option. It's always easier to remain confident in what you *can* do.

TAKE IT WITH YOU

No matter the match, no matter the outcome, you can and should take something away from the table with you (besides a cube of chalk). League and tournament matches offer the highest level of practice because you're playing under competitive conditions. This motivates you to be totally into the game at hand, trying to do your best. It's the best opportunity to practice these conditions, yet few players take the time after the match to analyze all but the most obvious—did they win or did they lose? There's a wealth of information waiting to be processed into your brain's computer, if you've paid attention.

The Thrill of Victory

You win a match, shake your opponent's hand, congratulate yourself, and look to see who you play next, all memory of the match instantly forgotten. You assume that since you won, all that no longer matters. It does. Run through this checklist each time you win to guarantee yourself a lesson from your victory:

1. **How did I feel?** Yes, of course you felt good. But carry that one step further. Visualize the end of the last game—your poise as you bent over the

game-winning shot, the confidence as you struck it, pure and true, sending the object ball crisply into the corner pocket. You rose from the shot, extended a victory fist into the air, and then humbly walked over to your opponent to shake hands and say, "Good game." Didn't that feel great? Of course it did! And you want to feel that way again and again. Holding that feeling close to you, owning it, will enable you to better visualize your next win.

2. **Did I play well?** A little tougher to answer honestly, isn't it? Perhaps you played terribly, but your opponent missed a few key shots and you capitalized on his misfortune. That's okay, and it's all part of the game. However, if you played poorly, you might want to take a moment to analyze where your game fell short and correct the mistakes in your mind before your next match. Your next opponent may not offer the same opportunities. Conversely, if you played the best pool you ever played in your life, you'll want to dwell on that, too. Remember each well-struck shot, carefully planned safety, and brilliantly executed run. The winning experience will do wonders for your confidence.

3. **Was I comfortable?** If so, what made you comfortable? Did fans or family nearby put you at ease? Were you on "home turf"? If you weren't comfortable, why? Were you paying too much attention to others watching the match? Were you hungry, thirsty, hot, or cold? Note the variables that made a difference in your match and carry them with you for future reference. Remember, when in competition, you want to re-create as many of the winning variables as possible to allow you to play your game and have fun.

4. **Was I focused or reckless?** Some players play better when they just let their games go, seeming to play without a care in the world. Others play better when their intensity could light a candle without a match. What were you thinking about? Were you distracted by a headache or a problem at home, or were you totally into the match? Gauging your level of intensity and your areas of focus in your wins will clue you in as to what type of player you are.

Lessons From Defeat

Yes, the agony of defeat. All players have experienced this one. It hurts, no matter how much fun they were having during the game. The initial reaction of typical players will often consist of the "shout and pout." They're sad, they're mad, they got robbed, they gave it away, they screwed up. No matter the reason for the loss, they're never playing this stupid game again. Luckily, people are resilient creatures. Twenty minutes later they're back to their normal selves, vowing to "get 'em next time." There's a fun, tongue-in-cheek saying among those who compete, "Some days you get the bear, and some days the bear gets you." While we don't advise saying this to your best friend 30 seconds after he has just lost a hill-hill match, we hope you get the point. Pool is a sport. Sports have winners, and losers. (Think of it this way: In a 128-player field, 1 person will win, and 127 others will go home the losers!) Nobody wins all the time. If they did, it would get boring. That's why people love underdogs.

It's true, nobody wants to lose, and it can be difficult to take a lesson from a tough loss that you don't want to dwell on, but you owe it to yourself to do just that. Again, make a mental checklist of what might have gone wrong. Focus on yourself, not your opponent. If she played perfect and never missed a ball, fine, the bear got you this time. But that's rare. Usually, there was something you could have done, somewhere in the match, to better your chances for success. Was your break weak? Did you go for a few crowd-pleasing shots and leave yourself tough instead of playing safe? Did you play your opponent and not the table? Did you lose your focus?

Keep in mind, you're not seeking excuses here. The goal is to find things that occurred that were in your control, things that you could have controlled better. If you learned just one thing—one safety, one pattern play, one strategic move, or one mental readjustment—then the match will not have been a total failure. Perhaps it was even the match that taught you that one thing that will take your game to the next level!

Good Sportsmanship

Above all, whatever else you take from the table, in victory or defeat, take your class and your dignity with you. Good sportsmanship isn't just about impressing the crowds. It's what defines you as a player. Shake your opponent's hand after the match, congratulate him on a game well played (whether he won or lost), and wish him luck on his next match or tournament.

Good sportsmanship isn't just about being polite—it will actually help your game. If you have played opponents who exhibit good sportsmanship, you respect them, don't you? They will equally respect you. At the same time, you can forget about acting up and focus on the task at hand, which is playing your best pool. You don't need the antics to win, and if you do, invest your time in practicing skills, not bad moves. Again, it's a game, it's meant to be fun, and you'll have more fun if you're a good sport.

Likewise, it's to your benefit to be a good sport, even when your opponent is exhibiting every bad habit he (or she) can dream up. If you lend fuel to his fire by reacting to his antics, he will benefit. Instead, play your game, the whole package, including the class act you bring to the table, and let him suffer on his own. He is obviously not having much fun. That's his problem, don't make it yours!

GOALS FOR IMPROVEMENT

You've heard it time and again, "You must have goals!" You need goals in your personal life, at work, and certainly in competition. And in order to have goals, you must have expectations. When you first get a taste of this game, you have no expectations. Making balls or missing balls has no bearing on your thoughts and feelings. Pool is fun. Playing pool is enough. The goal may be to have time to play more, but that's usually the extent of the desire.

Suddenly, you begin to improve. You become more proficient. You expect to make a few balls in a row. If you don't, you're angry or disappointed. You've made this shot before. You should always make it. Great expectations are double-edged swords. It's good to expect yourself to constantly improve, but bad if you assume you will automatically, and worse if you ever think you can "master" the sport.

Try to have one or two ultimate goals in mind for your game and write them down. Go ahead, think big. If you want to be a pro, by all means, that's what you want to write down. If you want to be the best player in your local league, that's great, too. If you want to win the world championships, outstanding!

But, keep in mind, the greater the goal, the more obstacles you will face on the way. If you just learned to play, and you have a job where you work 80 hours a week, obviously you'll have quite a challenge on your hands to compete on the pro tour within a year, let alone win the world championships.

Once you have your ultimate goals in mind, you can focus on the road that will get you there. It's easy to be realistic and set, for instance, a one-year goal to play in your first tournament and a five-year goal to play in your first pro event. This is sensible; it can be broken down into manageable, bite-size, short-range goals, and it can be achieved. Setting practical goals allows you to keep your promises. Being unrealistic makes it more difficult to set short-range goals to work up to your ultimate goal.

Let's look at specific ways you might set a pool goal. We'll stick with the example goal of competing on the pro tour five years from now. Financial and time obligations aside, you could have three short-range goals (along with specific steps to achieve each goal) that look like this:

1. Find a coach and get videotaped to find trouble spots: (a) Contact the Billiard Congress of America to find the closest certified instructor, (b) combine your vacation with a visit to one of the professional pool schools (World champion Allison Fisher runs several each year), (c) watch at least three instruction tapes to round out your learning.

2. Up weekly practice to four times per week, at least 2 hours each practice: (a) One practice each week against Bob, the local pro at ABC Billiards, (b) two practices working on run-outs by yourself, (c) one practice dedicated to top-shelf shots and safety strategies.

3. Compete in qualifiers for professional tour stops, or enter a city or state championship: (a) Practice playing under tournament conditions with a coach or in weekly league play, (b) build confidence for events with targeted practices, half offensive, half defensive, (c) spend 10 minutes a day visualizing a perfect run-out and tournament match win!

There's no right or wrong way to do this. Some players will put emphasis on their mental game: expanding their knowledge by watching pro events on TV, viewing matches on videotape, reading instruction books, or getting a coach. Others will simply want to hone physical skills and make it a goal to play at least an hour every day to develop consistency. The important thing is to design a plan. Just like your plan of attack on the pool table, the bigger picture—your plan of attack for your ultimate pool goal—will benefit with a set of steps to get there.

At the risk of offering you yet another uncomfortable flashback to school days, remember when the teacher made you write your spelling words 10 times each? You hated it, didn't you? But the underlying concept (for the few of us that paid attention) wasn't so bad. Writing down your pool goals is a good way to remember them. We know some pros who actually carry a pool journal with them, writing down where and when they practiced, what they achieved, and what still needs work in the next session.

Writing down goals is also vital for two other reasons. First, it serves as a sort of contract for you. When a goal is written down, it becomes real. This promise you've made to yourself becomes tangible when it is something you can see on paper, rather than an abstract thought floating around an already crowded brain full of thoughts. Since each day is made up of so many choices, this makes it easier to stick to your pool goal of practicing for an extra hour, for example, instead of turning on the TV or playing a video game.

Second, writing down goals makes it easier to tweak them (expanding or shrinking them as you go) and to monitor your progress on the way. For example, you may set the goal to play an hour a day. But by the third week, you may realize you haven't got a prayer of playing on Saturdays—it's your only day to get everything else done, from bathing the dog to mowing the lawn. You can adjust, either by adding a few minutes of practice on to your other days or simply revising the goal to play an hour a day, *six* days a week.

Chances are, every short-term goal can be adjusted to meet your needs and still be a rung on the ladder to your ultimate goal.

Finally, don't force yourself into a mold that doesn't fit. If you have a goal to practice 2 hours a day, and an hour into your practice session you're paying no attention to your shots and hating every minute of your practice, you're obviously not doing yourself any good. Adjust down to a level that works for you, even if it's only 20 minutes a day. When you are learning difficult pool concepts, 20 minutes is often the maximum attention span your mind and body will have before wandering. If you want to work up to that 2-hour mark, then do it in tiny increments, a few minutes a week, until those 2 hours fly by and you can't wait for more time at the table.

Setting goals that you hate or that will ultimately frustrate you won't be of any immediate or long-term benefit. If you can't stand playing safeties, you certainly need to put some time into them, but scheduling a full practice session of safeties will only bore you and cause you to lose interest in the game. You won't be able to keep your goal, you'll break the promise you made to yourself, and you'll do your best to lose the piece of paper on which you wrote all those "pipe dream" goals. Instead, make goals as easy as possible to achieve and exceed. Make it your goal to play just 15 minutes a day. Stop yourself at 20. You've exceeded your goal, and you wish you could play more. Increase your goals in slow but steady increments, so you'll always be improving.

Becoming a player isn't just about practice or attitude or confidence. It's about combining all your strengths, physical and mental, offensive and defensive, in order to become a "whole" player. Set your short and long term goals to reflect improvement steps in those physical and mental skills you need. By developing these skills together you will become a better player and get the most out of your game.

Expert 8-Ball

8-Ball is one of the most well-known and widely played games on the green felt. Even people who don't really know pool know the game of stripes and solids. It's how most shooters begin their cueing careers. What makes the game so popular? It's a simple game wrapped in complexity.

The objective and the rules are simple. There are 15 balls: 7 stripes, 7 solids, and 1 black ball (the eight ball). Pocket your group of balls and then shoot the black in and you win. You can play one-on-one, with partners, or in a scotch doubles format. Yet, the more you dig into the game, the more complex it becomes. There are intricacies in pattern play, timing, and offensive and defensive strategies. Players have the opportunity to use their intellect, imagination, and the most advanced shooting skills they possess in this simple game of stripes and solids. In part 2 of this book, we help the player develop skills in the three distinct parts of the 8-Ball game—the opening game (including the break), the middle game, and the end game. Each part of the game requires different talents and strategies to maintain that competitive edge.

The early part of the game, or the opening, is as important in 8-Ball as it is in other games of strategy, such as chess. This is where your direction is determined, where your path is set. It is here that you determine whether that path leads to victory or defeat. Deciding which group of balls to claim, and whether to run or hide—and when—are all determined in the early part of the game. You should always begin the opening with the end in mind.

The middle game brings about the heart of play. This is where the rubber meets the road, where you apply all that you have learned about shot making, cue ball control, and strategy. We will add to that stock some intricacies specific to successful 8-Ball.

The end game is where you bring it all home. When the opening and middle games are played well, the end game is simply where you close the door on your opponent. But often the end game becomes a battlefield as each player is waiting for the other to make a mistake.

6

8-Ball Openers

Your first step in the opening of any 8-Ball game should be coming to the table prepared. The game begins with a power break and subsequent selection of a group of balls. Here you find future obstacles and make decisions about how and when to overcome them. The opening shot after the break is crucial and unique in that, since the table is open (depending on the house rules), the choices are limitless.

In order to develop an effective strategy, you must know the many aspects of the competition in which you are about to engage. Assessments should always be the first matter of business in any serious competition. In 8-Ball, you must understand your own capabilities, those of your opponent, and the environment in which you're playing. What tools do you possess that will allow you to achieve victory? These tools include mechanical fundamentals, shot-making skills, and your ability to imagine and think clearly under pressure. You must know what you are capable of doing as well as what you are *not* capable of doing. You cannot possibly have a winning strategy without knowing your strengths and weaknesses. You cannot perform a proper risk assessment without intimate knowledge of your own skills.

You should also know your opponent's strengths and weaknesses for the same reasons. Professional football coaches spend hours on end reviewing game films to prepare for Sunday's battle. What do you know about your opponent? Each opponent has a unique set of skills and will react differently in different situations.

Finally, what about the environment? Are you playing on big tables or bar tables? Is the cloth slow or fast? Is the cue ball oversized or overweighted? Are the tables too close together or are they a comfortable distance apart? How will the equipment affect your strategy or that of your opponent?

THE BREAK

The break is one of the most important shots in the game. Some would argue it is *the* most important. It sets the stage for the rest of the game. It determines whether your next shot will be a nightmare or a dream come true. It determines whether or not you will have a next shot!

In 8-Ball, you should use the power break. The object of the power break is to pocket at least one ball while scattering the rest of the balls as much as possible. When scattered, the remaining balls can be pocketed more easily than if clustered in small groups around the table. The rack is very important in achieving a good ball spread. In an 8-Ball rack, be sure that the stripes and solids are alternated throughout the rack as much as possible. If the balls are not alternated in this fashion, you may end up with clusters of like balls. In addition, ensure that the two wing balls are not both stripes or solids, since they are the two balls most frequently pocketed.

In many formats, the privilege to break is earned by winning the previous game. In order to string racks together and impose some kind of mental anguish on your opponent, you must have a solid break. Breaking the balls without pocketing one is like being all dressed up with nowhere to go but back to your chair.

Achieving a great break is a matter of directing enough force through the racked balls to get them to move about the table in such a way that one or more falls into a pocket and the others are spread nicely for future conquest. There are two important factors in this equation—power and contact.

Some people think you have to hit the rack at 100 miles an hour to get a good break. The fact of the matter is that the top cue ball speed of professionals tested reached only 31 miles an hour. Even so, those high-speed breaks had a tendency to mishit the target ball and fly off the table. You must achieve a solid hit on the target ball in order to transfer all that energy to the pack.

Lining It Up

In order to get yourself into good position for a solid break, you need to do a number of things. First, take a slightly wider stance than usual. This will allow more power and spring in your upper body. Place at least 60 percent of your body weight on your front leg so you can rock your body forward on the shot and increase the cue stick speed. Also, stand up a little taller on the shot to give your swinging arm more room. This will enhance your follow-through. Next, adjust your grip and bridge placement. For the break shot, you should move your grip hand back on the cue stick and increase your bridge length about the same distance—a distance that allows the forearm to still be nearly vertical at the moment of impact on the cue ball. This will naturally allow you to have more cue stick with which to follow through. Keep your cue stick tip very near the cue ball—about an inch away. This helps the tip find its way to the spot on the cue ball you want it to contact. You may also need to change the way you bridge. It's easier to follow through with an open bridge. In fact, if you use a closed bridge, you will find that you have to open it up to allow for the proper follow-through anyway. Begin with whatever feels comfortable to you.

Keep your back hand as loose as possible while still maintaining control over the cue stick. This is the key to an explosive break. A loose hold allows the wrist to accelerate through the shot, speeding the cue stick through the cue ball as it does. For those of you who play golf, you will recognize the similarities: The lighter the hold on the club, the more club head speed is generated.

Turn your back hip toward the shot. While your normal stance is more likely to have your hips angled at 45 degrees, to get more power on the break shot, square them up. In other words, if you are right handed, as you execute the shot, turn your right hip toward the rack.

Getting a Solid Hit

If you are not getting a solid hit on the rack, then only a fraction of the force you have applied to the cue ball is being transferred to the rack. Another side effect is that the cue ball has retained that energy, so instead of stopping in the center of the table it continues to bounce around at the mercy of the pool gods, or it flies off the table, endangering the health of the people around you.

On most shots, you will sight the object ball last before you propel the cue ball toward it. However, on the break shot, you may find it better to sight the cue ball just before you pull the trigger. The reason for this is when you look at the cue ball last you will create more of a stunning action on the cue ball. If you look at the target ball last, you will create more follow-through. The stunned cue ball is less likely to carry with it any spin that will detract from the transfer of energy to the rack.

Building Power

Once you have mastered a solid hit on the target ball, you can build up the power in your stroke. Develop your break by exerting just 20 percent of your hit strength, similar to a slow or medium hit on the cue ball. Slowly build up the speed of your stroke. When you hit four or five solid breaks in a row, step up to 40, 60, and 80 percent of your strength in a similar fashion. Most players will settle in the 70 to 80 percent range. Avoid digging your cue tip into the table bed while performing your break stroke. This has a tendency to slow down the speed of the cue stick. You also risk breaking the spine of the shaft, making it more likely to warp.

Making the Break

Place the cue ball along either side rail in the kitchen (just behind the head string) and aim for the second ball in the rack, that is, the ball just behind the head ball. Use a below center hit on the cue ball lest it become a flying object. By hitting the second ball solidly, two good things are likely to happen. First, you will get a good spread on the balls, and second, the cue ball will come

---

Break Practice

The break shot is an all-important shot that deserves some practice time. In addition to stepping up the power in your break described earlier, use the following technique to practice getting a solid hit on the cue ball. This exercise requires a cue ball with a dot or circle on it. Place the cue ball so that the dot or circle is at the point of center ball and lined up with the target ball in the rack. Now really scuff up your cue tip with chalk so that when the tip contacts the cue ball, the chalk will leave an imprint for you to analyze. Have a friend grab the cue ball as quickly as possible after contact with the rack. Examine the cue ball and notice where the chalk has made its mark in relation to the dot or circle. Did you hit center ball? If you are not hitting the cue ball where you want, try sighting the cue ball last before pulling the trigger. When you can consistently hit your mark this way, you can revert to sighting the target ball on the stroke. Another option used by some professionals is to sight a ball in the rack directly behind the target ball. This facilitates an effective follow-through.

---

back into the center of the table ensuring that you get a good shot to start your run. This break shot carries an added bonus of enabling you to make the eight ball on the break more frequently.

However, a break shot that uses the head ball can also be quite effective. It is still critical to get a solid hit on the target ball. Aiming at the head ball is advantageous because it is a bigger target. You can get a full hit whether your cue ball is in the center of the table or all the way to the side rail. The cue ball can be controlled more easily with a frontal attack, since it is a more straight-on shot.

STRIPES OR SOLIDS

Unlike 9-Ball, where the order of ball pocketing is predetermined, in 8-Ball you can pocket the balls in any order, using many different sequences. The options are often overwhelming to all but the seasoned professional. Here's a thought process that will help you make your decision on stripes or solids:

1. Look at the eight ball. This may seem backward and it is. 8-Ball is a game of thinking backward. You must have the end game in mind from the very beginning. So, first look at the eight ball. Do you have a clear path to a pocket? Is there a clear path once one of the ball groups has been removed? What balls, if any, are close to the eight ball? Do any provide a natural angle to get position on the eight ball? If so, this group would be a good choice. In figure 6.1, the eight ball has a clear path to either corner pocket at the bottom of the figure. You have both stripe and solid options to get position on the eight.

2. Which group of balls will give you the best opportunity to run the table? Carefully look at both groups, observing any hidden traps or clusters that would prove difficult to open. If the balls are wide open, find either a ball close to the eight ball or a ball that provides a shot with a natural angle to get position on the eight ball. This is called the *key ball*.

Referring back to figure 6.1, two stripes are tied up between the corner and side pocket on the left side of the table, but the solids are wide open. In the opening shot, given an equal opportunity to pocket either group, the solids are preferred.

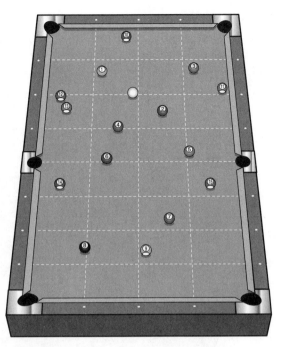

Figure 6.1 Choosing stripes or solids should be based on careful forethought.

3. Work your way back from the key ball to the opening shot. In figure 6.1, the seven ball is a good key ball. It is the only solid ball on the same side of the table as the eight, so it makes sense to work your way down to that end of the table. Moving the cue ball as little as possible minimizes your risk. Thinking backward from the seven ball to the six, five, four, three, two, and then one happens to represent a natural stop-out (in numerical order for sake of illustration). In figure 6.2, we've removed the striped balls to show you just how easy this run-out looks.

4. Have a plan. The most important thing in 8-Ball is pattern play. All too often we have seen players end a run simply because they hadn't

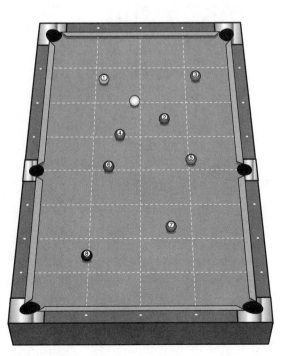

Figure 6.2 A run with solids.

thought the whole thing through adequately *before* they began. Their shots keep getting more and more difficult until they are asking themselves to do the impossible. Of equal frequency are players who get out of line because they haven't decided whether to take the next shot in the side or the corner. Suddenly, they're faced with a bank shot. Start with a plan, but be willing to change it if the conditions of the table change.

Whether playing 9-Ball or 8-Ball, Efren Reyes is known for his sharpshooting skills and incredible position play.

TAKE YOUR SHOT

Once you've run through your assessment, it's time to move. Just as in a well-planned game of chess, the opening shots will be critical. Let's look at an example. In figure 6.3, you have an opening shot opportunity to break up the twelve-two cluster using either a stripe or a solid. Which is the best choice? Go back to your assessment process to help you decide.

The eight ball has a clear path to the top right corner only. However, it is surrounded by two stripes, which means that if you take stripes, those balls will obviously be gone

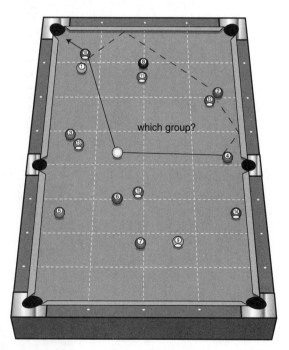

Figure 6.3 8-Ball run-outs are made easier by careful planning.

before you shoot the eight. Thinking ahead, the eight ball actually has a clear path to either top corner.

If you look at the solids, the three, one, and two are all in trouble. Your opening shot can break out the two ball but leave you with two more trouble spots to deal with later. Looking back at the stripes, the thirteen ball is near the three, though it has a clear path to the side pocket. Granted, it is the only pocket available, but there are two balls on that side of the table that may be used to get shape on it. All things considered, when you take the ten ball first and open up the twelve ball, the stripes become a viable route to victory. Cut the ten in the corner with a medium hit, using a touch of right english to ensure that you clear the eight ball and come into the two ball first. As long as you hit the two ball first, you will open up the balls effectively. If you hit the twelve ball, you run a greater risk of pushing the balls together or moving the twelve to a place where the two obstructs a clear shot in the corner. After the break-out there are two insurance balls—the eleven and the thirteen—to facilitate your continued run.

Sometimes it's difficult to make the right decision because one or more of the balls from the *wrong* group were made on the break. In figure 6.4, you would be tempted to take the solids because two were made on the break. However, the table layout dictates that you must take the stripes. Even with the five ball available for the opening shot, the table doesn't provide an easy way to get to the trouble ball (four). The stripes pose no difficulties from the break and offer *many* different ways to run out. One example is as follows: 14, right top corner; 13, left top corner; 9, right top corner; 10, left bottom corner; 15, right side; 12, left top corner; 11, left top corner; 8, right side.

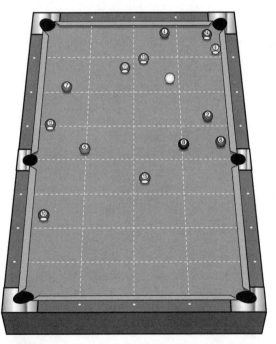

Figure 6.4 In this situation the solids look like the better option since there are fewer on the table, but stripes are the smarter play.

Opening Clusters

Since the game of 8-Ball puts all 15 balls in play, it is very common to have to deal with clusters. This can happen in the beginning, middle, or end game. Whenever it happens, you need to think about the same things. Don't be tempted to take a shot at a break-out the first chance you get. Look for your *best chance.* You may have to play position leading up to the most effective break-out shot.

Next, you need to think about how the cluster will react to the break-out. The break-out may take place with an object ball you drive into the pack or with the cue ball itself. In either case, think through the point of contact and the reaction of the balls. What side of the pack do you need to hit? Where will the balls go? Given the intended point of contact, will you be tying up the cue ball or will it clear?

The most common mistake people make in breaking up clusters is to hit the shot too hard. The misconception is that they must move the clustered balls around a lot to set them free. The fact is that most clusters need only be nudged to open them enough for play. When you hit the cluster too hard, you run the risk of moving the balls into new trouble spots.

Finally, you need to think about an *insurance ball.* An insurance ball is one that is in such a place that it can be pocketed from almost any position. This ball acts as insurance in case the ball you are breaking out doesn't move into the makeable position you had desired.

In figure 6.5, your opponent has not made a ball on the break. The cue ball is left close to the center of the table. The eight ball is just off the foot rail with a clear path to either corner pocket. Either a stripe or solid can provide you that key ball with a natural angle to the eight. The problem in this rack is found in a cluster near the left side pocket, along with a blocked ten and four ball near the right corner. However, the stripes provide more natural opportunities to break up the clusters than the solids do. Therefore, stripes are the best choice.

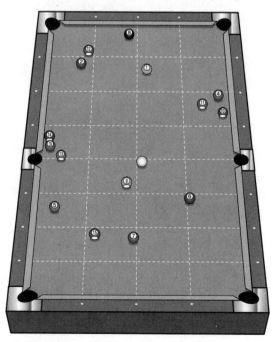

Figure 6.5 Stripes provide better opportunities to break up troublesome clusters.

The best opening shot here involves making the thirteen ball in the side pocket and breaking out the fourteen in the same shot. One way to execute this shot is to use the cue ball to nudge the balls after making contact with the thirteen, and the second option is to pocket the thirteen off the three ball. The problem with the first option is that if you drive the cue ball into the fourteen, you run the risk of not having a good shot after that. You might knock the fourteen toward the middle of the table to get a shot at it in the side. You also might get a shot on the nine or fifteen, but this is all very risky. On the other hand, if you make the thirteen off the three, as shown in figure 6.6, you have an *insurance* opportunity to continue your run with either the nine or the fifteen ball. (More on insurance balls in the following chapter.) When you make the thirteen off the three, you expect the fourteen ball to head toward the corner pocket, clearing the three. And since you don't have to hit the shot hard, you can expect the three ball to stay close to where it is. Most important, with this shot you can control the cue ball. When you draw the cue ball back a little, you can expect to have the nine ball in the corner for your next shot, but if you don't like that angle, you also have the option of the fifteen with an angle to take you back toward the middle of the table. Whatever happens, because the table layout is changing, you will need to reassess your run-out pattern to find the most natural way to the eight ball.

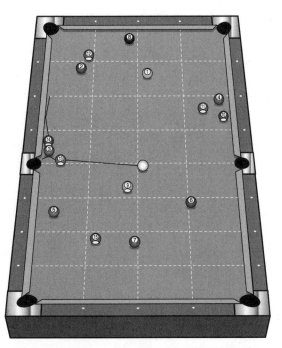

Figure 6.6 By pocketing the thirteen, you can clear your way to an easier run-out.

In figure 6.7, all the trouble for this layout is found at the top left corner of the table. The table is still open, but four balls surround the eight. Everything else looks relatively easy. This opening shot requires that you pocket the ten ball and break open the nearby cluster. The one-ten combination will drive the one ball into the cluster with a full hit on the fourteen. (A combination using a ball from each group can only be used

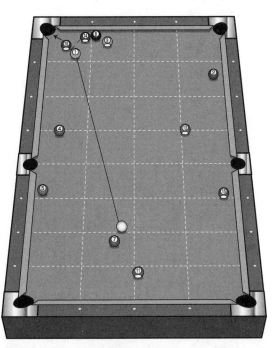

Figure 6.7 With the table open, you can pocket the ten ball and break up the cluster to have an easier run-out opportunity.

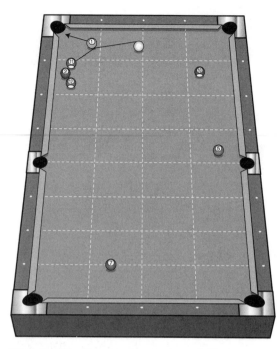

Figure 6.8 Breaking up a three-ball cluster.

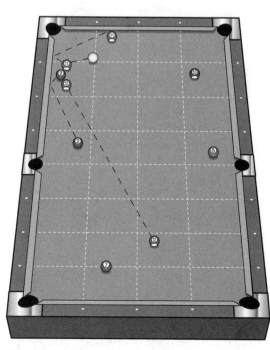

Figure 6.9 A solid hit on the eleven ball ensures the best break-up.

when the table is still "open.") Hit this shot firm enough to clear both striped balls. Be sure to control the cue ball with a stop shot so that you'll have an insurance shot on the thirteen ball in the event your other options are less favorable when the balls stop rolling.

Knowing *how* to open up clusters is a strong asset. When hitting into a cluster, most of the energy is transferred to the first ball contacted, which then transfers energy to other balls in the clump. Most often just a little bump into the balls will be enough to open a cluster sufficiently and offer a shot at the opened balls. If you have plenty of room to work with (meaning you won't be creating more clusters by moving the balls too far), a firm rap can be played.

Opening clusters is an art that can be learned by simple observation and experience. Feel and touch will be developed in time. The best way to learn cluster busting is by playing straight pool, where you are regularly forced to open the balls from a full-rack position. Figure 6.8 shows a three-ball cluster that must be broken up. Cutting the one ball to the right side of the pocket will ensure a solid, full-ball hit on the eleven ball. In doing this you make sure the two ball gets bumped clear of the striped balls. If you just glance the eleven ball, there's no guarantee the two ball will move at all. Figure 6.9 shows the outcome of a full hit on the eleven ball.

Using Combinations

In figure 6.10, your opponent has not pocketed any balls on the break. You may assess the table as follows:

- The eight ball currently has no pocket. The five ball prevents a clear path to the corner, making it difficult to see from the other side as well.
- The striped balls have a cluster of three near the middle of the table with limited choices for break-out.
- The solids are wide open, with the exception of the five ball, which is difficult to cut in the corner pocket because of its proximity to the eight.

Given these circumstances, your best group is the solids and your best shot is to play the thirteen-eight-five combination in the corner. This claims the solid group, pockets your only trouble ball, and clears the pocket for the eight ball.

Keep the rest of the rack in mind to have a shot after the opening. Keep the movement of the first balls (the thirteen and eight balls) to a minimum. You don't want to tie up the eight ball elsewhere, since you will need to pocket it in the near future.

Shoot the combination using a soft to medium hit with the idea of moving the cue ball into the landing zone shown in figure 6.11. By positioning the cue ball

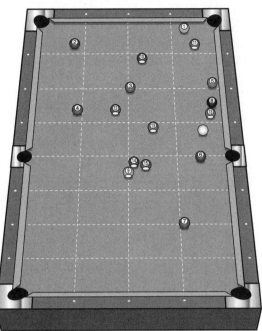

Figure 6.10 A well-played combination shot can give you the better option to play solids instead of stripes.

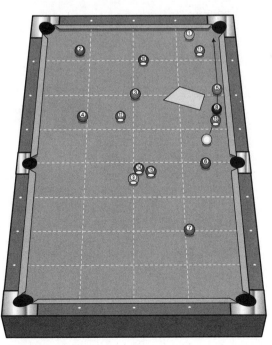

Figure 6.11 Note the landing zone for the cue ball.

Area Position

There are times when you may want to play "area position" in 8-Ball to allow for a choice of shots instead of playing for one particular shot. This keeps your options open. In order to get the most bang for your positioning buck, there is no payoff as welcome as that when you find your cue ball in the center of the table.

In addition to having lots of options from the center, you'll find that the center of the table is a place where you never have to jack up (as when on the rail), so you are not restricted in applying spin. You never have a very long shot, and you seldom have to use the mechanical bridge.

In figure 6.12a, you want to pocket the one ball in the upper left-hand corner and draw the cue ball to the middle of the table. From there you'll have a shot at virtually every other solid ball on the table. Bonus: All along the cue ball path (the dotted line) are options for shots, so you have decreased your reliance on speed. When attempting area position, it's still a good idea to have a specific destination in mind, so pick a particular ball to shoot next and a particular spot on the table for your target position. Once the cue ball comes to rest, assess your situation and

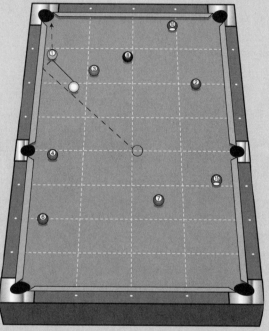

Figure 6.12a By pocketing the one, you'll have a shot at nearly every solid.

determine your run-out plan before moving on. Remember to be flexible and let the table show you the most natural pattern to play.

The game in figure 6.12b has quite a few more balls left in play, but the center of the table is still a great place to be for the player with solids. Pocket the seven with a firm center ball hit to move the cue ball two rails back into the middle of the action. All balls are in play from there. Again, have a specific next shot in mind, particularly if one shot is tougher to get position on than others or has limited pocket options. (In this illustration, you might want to position for the five ball next for a 5, 2, 4, 3, 1, 8 run-out.)

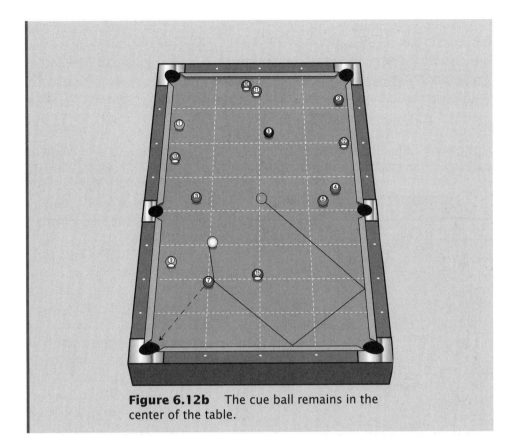

Figure 6.12b The cue ball remains in the center of the table.

there, you have several options for the next shot, the most desirable of which will be the two in the corner. Your pattern will be largely dictated by where the eight ball lands, since you will need to find your key ball and work backward from there. With the soft to medium, full hit on the second ball, however, you can rest assured that the eight will not venture far from the spot behind where it contacts the five ball.

Opening game combination opportunities will be plentiful in many 8-Ball games. It pays to know how to play them to keep your advantage at the table on subsequent shots.

Practicing Pattern Plays

A good way to practice your opening game pattern play is to throw out just the solid (or stripe) balls and the eight ball. See how many different patterns you can find. They are numerous. Some are easier than others, of course. Some are more natural for right-handers than left-handers. Once you have a good feel for the simple patterns when the table is wide open, throw all 15 balls on the table, take ball-in-hand, and find the best patterns there.

Another great practice routine is playing a "call" 8-Ball game where you must call *the next* ball and its intended pocket *before* you shoot your current shot. No matter what happens, you must stick to your original call. This forces you to really plan ahead!

SAFETY PLAYS

Sometimes you will go through your opening game assessment and come to the realization that it just doesn't make sense to pocket a ball after the break.

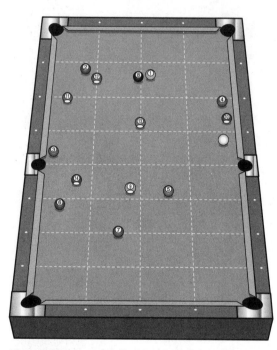

It's time to look for a viable safety. In figure 6.13, you may assess the table and determine the following:

The eight ball is still near the spot it was racked at the foot of the table, and the nearby one ball takes away the right corner pocket. At the same time, the eight ball prevents the one ball from having any pocket at that end of the table at all. Further, two more stripe-solid couples are making any kind of run-out a difficult proposition. The best play here is a safe one.

Whenever you play a safe shot, you want to keep a couple of things in mind. Obviously, you won't want to leave your opponent a shot. This is more difficult in 8-Ball

Figure 6.13 A well-played safe is key to winning this rack.

when the table is still open. Your opponent can hit any ball to make a legal shot. In such a case, you need to use a "if I do that, he can do that" strategy to think ahead to all the possibilities.

The second thing you want to accomplish, if at all possible, is to move the balls into a more favorable position for your future shots. Again, with an open table this is not easy. You run the risk of placing one group in a more favorable position only to have them claimed by your opponent.

In figure 6.14, two good options for an opening safety are shown. In shot A, you shoot the one ball full, sending it past the eight ball, and you use just enough speed and a touch of high ball to move the cue ball to the foot rail. The one ball moves two rails, rebounding between the two and eleven as shown. This shot accomplishes four things. First, you leave the cue ball where your opponent does not have a clear shot at pocketing a ball. Next, you clear the eight ball so that both corner pockets are now available. Third, you open up the one ball, which had no pocket. Fourth, you place the one ball in such a position that it can be used to break up the two-twelve cluster, or get position on the short side of the two if necessary later in the rack. So, you have made the solid balls more desirable yet have not left your opponent with a way to claim them. The difficulty in this shot comes from having to control the speed and direction of both the cue ball and the one ball.

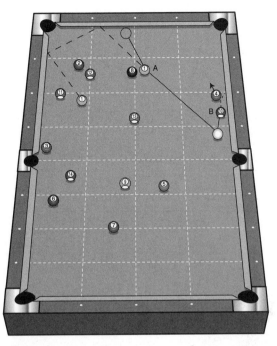

Figure 6.14 Shot B is the easier safe, but shot A accomplishes more.

Shot B is an easier safe to execute but does not accomplish all the objectives that are realized in shot A. Roll the cue ball into the ten with just enough speed for the cue ball to hit the rail after contact. This will leave your opponent in a tough spot. Your opponent may take the difficult shot on the nine ball, but if the cue ball is tied up with the ten ball, the cueing options are few. Further, the ten, twelve, and eight ball are still tied up with limited break-out options.

As you can see, the opening of any 8-Ball game isn't just about busting the balls wide open. After executing the power break, you'll kick your strategy right into high gear, deciding which group of balls to pocket, how you'll execute a run-out, or how you'll play a safety that will get you back to the table. Remember, those decisions will be affected by your environment, your opponent's game, and your own strengths and weaknesses.

7

Mid-Game Strategy

The middle game is where all the action takes place. It's the main course, where you get to use all those great shots and strategies, and where you can let your imagination run wild. In the middle game, you must be able to get to your key ball, find and use insurance balls, open up clusters, move flawlessly around obstacles, and come up with a game-saving safety when needed.

THE KEY BALL

We emphasized that in the opening of the game, you need to already have your end game in mind. And it should remain on your mind in the middle game. In the opening, you identify a key ball to get shape on the eight ball, and in the middle game, you'll be working your way to that key ball. Caution: Do not be tempted to pocket your key ball prematurely. You may find yourself looking for an easy shot to feel confident about your game and your chances of winning. That key ball will look mighty appealing. Don't be taken in. It will just make things harder down the road. One pool player we know began to run a rack of 8-Ball with so little forethought that by the time he got to his last two balls he was in quite a predicament. After studying his options, he got down and shot the *eight ball* straight in the side pocket, claiming it was the only shot he had.

In figure 7.1, you have solids and your opponent has left the cue ball in an advantageous spot for you. You had previously identified the one ball as your key ball, since it offers the most natural lead in to the eight. You can imagine a triangular target area for the cue ball following the shot on the one ball. The points of the triangle will be at approximately the eight ball, the corner pocket, and just in front of the one ball. Working backward, you could probably get

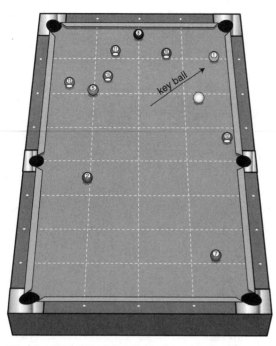

Figure 7.1 Work backward to get to your key object ball before the eight ball.

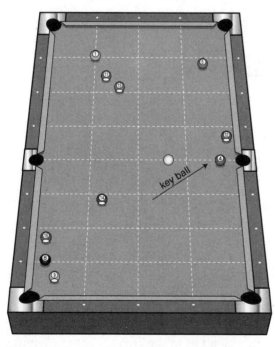

Figure 7.2 Imagine where you must be to get a good shot on the eight ball to determine where you want to be after shooting the key ball.

there from any of the other three balls on the table, but movement from the five ball to position on the one seems the easiest. You would be happy with all but the sharpest cuts to the left for position here, but you would prefer something with just a slight angle to the right or left of the one ball so you don't have to spin the cue ball and complicate the shot.

Working your way backward from the five to the two and the two to the seven, you open your final inning by pocketing the seven ball in the corner, and the cue ball travels one rail to position on the two. For the best position on the five, you prefer to be straight in on the two ball. A stop shot from here will give you a natural angle to swing across the table and get that shape you want on the one ball.

To facilitate this run, pocket the seven with a touch of inside (left) english. This keeps the cue ball on the wide end of the target area and takes a little speed off the cue ball so it won't roll past the side pockets.

Even precarious positions have their solutions with the use of a key ball. Take a look at figure 7.2. Your opponent just missed the nine ball, and now both the nine and fifteen are making it difficult for you to see the eight. Luckily, you have the four ball in the side, which provides a good key ball for an otherwise tough spot. You must take the five ball first, because you cannot see the one, and you need to keep the four ball for your key ball if at all possible.

Knowing that the four ball is the key ball, you should work backward from the four to the one to the five. Determine how to shoot the five to leave yourself an angle on the one (an angle that will then move the cue ball into position for the four). Start by imagining the area where the cue ball must be in order to have a good shot on the eight. Then determine the target area for position on the four and on the one. This must all be done before you take your first shot at the five. Remember, you must think a minimum of three balls ahead. You should be able to cut the one ball to the right to get the angle you need to move the cue ball into position for the four. So, hit the five in the corner with a stop shot. Next, cut the one ball in with a middle left hit and medium to slow speed to bring the cue ball into the center of the table. Be careful not to travel past the side pocket or you may have to move the cue ball eight feet instead of eight inches on your next shot! If you fall short of the middle of the table, it's no problem. You can still easily get to your target area for position. Pocket the four with a stop shot and you leave a good shot on the eight in the corner.

Let's say you're tempted to take the four ball first. There is a way out. The one ball becomes your key ball, but the shot is much more difficult. Now you have to move your cue ball more, which is always risky business. You must have pinpoint accuracy off the one to move the cue ball into position on the other end of the table for the eight.

There are many roads that will take you to the eight ball in most racks, but your objective is always to find the easiest way. In figure 7.3, your opponent has cleared most of the striped balls from the table, and your solids are all wide open. One way to simplify your travel is to clear one end of the table and then the other. This minimizes the total distance your cue ball must move, decreasing your reliance on speed control.

Here, you could start with the four ball and clear the top end of the table before working your way to the bottom half of the table. A good sequence could be the 4, 5, 3, 1, 2. After you clear the top half of the table, your next objective will be to get a

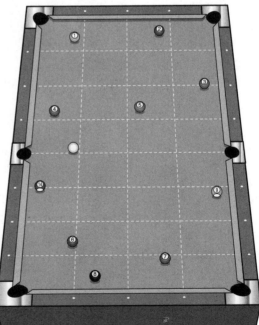

Figure 7.3 Working your eight-ball pattern play from one end of the table to the other proves easiest in this rack.

relatively straight angle on the six ball for an easy stop shot and position on the seven ball, and then to stop for the eight in the low left corner pocket. Again, thinking from the eight ball to your first shot can reduce cue ball travel.

CLEARING A POCKET

At the risk of stating the obvious, in order to run the table, you must have a clear pocket for each ball you wish to make. In 8-Ball, there are many times when your opponent is kind enough to miss a shot, but that missed shot *invariably* hangs in the pocket, preventing one or more of your balls from finding an easy home.

Thus, it will pay to become proficient at clearing your opponent's balls from a pocket. You can achieve this with a combination, a carom, or, though less common in today's rules, an illegal hit. The situation in figure 7.4 is best addressed with a carom shot. A soft shot to the left edge of the ten ball pockets the two,

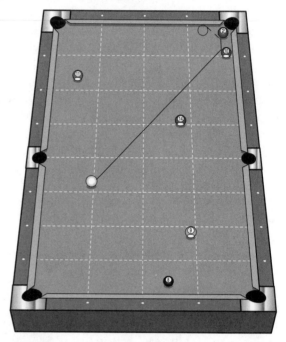

Figure 7.4 Clearing a blocked pocket with the use of a top-shelf carom shot.

and the cue ball lands at or near the short rail. Both the fourteen and nine ball block the eight ball from a direct hit. Had you chosen the combination, the cue ball would have been more difficult to control and keep on the right half of the table, increasing the chance that your opponent would get a shot on the eight. Similarly, illegally pocketing the two would have no benefit in this situation, as many leagues employ the ball-in-hand rule on any foul.

Figure 7.5 calls for a combination to clear the one ball from the pocket. The eight ball is blocking the other pocket, and it is not advisable to try a break-out shot given the lay of the table. You'll want to pocket the one ball with the ten so that the ten follows it into the pocket. The key to making this happen is to transfer enough topspin to the ten ball so that after the initial contact with the one, the ten will continue to roll into the pocket. To transfer the maximum amount of topspin, you will need a full hit on the ten. Play the twelve ball first, as shown, to get as straight in as possible for the combination shot. Shoot the ten with a below center hit on the cue ball. This will translate to topspin on the object ball. At the right speed, the cue ball stops in position for the eight in the opposite corner.

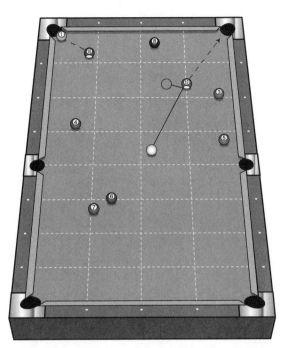

Figure 7.5 Clearing a blocked pocket with a combination shot.

Clearing Your Own Group

There are times when you will have to clear balls in your own group from a pocket in order to pocket other balls in the group. By pocketing one of your balls, you will be able to use that same pocket later to continue your run. Working through your run-out pattern, you will find that certain balls must be taken early to open up the pocket to your other balls.

Figure 7.6 shows that the ten ball should be pocketed first to run the table. Once the ten ball is pocketed in the corner, the pocket will be open for the twelve ball to be played there. If not, you'll be forced to play the twelve-ten combination later in the run-out, a much tougher shot.

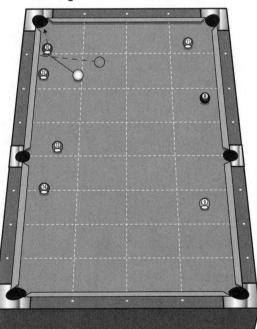

Figure 7.6 Pocketing the right balls of your group first allows you to open the pocket for other balls in your group.

In figure 7.7, you can see how clearing your own group can also be accomplished with a clever carom shot. In shot A, the five ball is blocking the ten ball in the upper right-hand corner. By pocketing the nine ball off the five, you open that pocket so the ten can be made there in the future. Shot B shows the nine ball coming off the long rail into the six ball, gently moving the six out of the way of the ten; the ten can then be made in the same pocket as the nine.

Take a Foul?

Yes, in rare cases, taking a foul is a necessary evil, no matter the ball-in-hand rules of your particular league. In figure 7.8, intentionally pocketing your opponent's nine ball clears the pocket for the two balls you've got left on that side of the table. At the same time, since the eight ball is clustered within those balls, even with ball-in-hand, your opponent will have no shot on the eight. Your opponent will have to contact the eight to avoid committing a foul, and this will likely result in moving your balls enough to get a better shot to the newly cleared pocket. Even if your opponent takes an intentional foul, you'll have ball-in-hand and can force your opponent into a three-foul situation or a wild shot that will definitely break up your cluster.

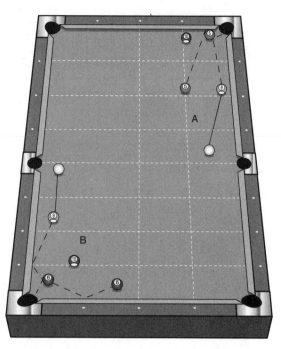

Figure 7.7 Clearing the line to a pocket with a carom shot, you'll be in better shape to pocket the ten ball.

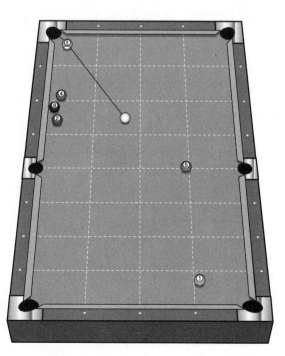

Figure 7.8 Example of a strategic intentional foul.

Practice Offense With "99"

Playing a cue sport game that results in a score, and a subsequent average of scores, provides a way for you to track your progress and set personal goals to reach even higher skill levels. The game of "99" offers just that, along with another bonus. Because you are simply breaking and attempting to run nine racks of nine balls, you will begin to quickly learn offensive patterns and to realize when, in actual match play, a safety would be your best bet!

Several BCA certified instructors have adopted "99" as a teaching tool, and room owners across the country are using the game in local tournaments. There's also a Pool & Billiard Rated Player International membership in this program that enables you to track averages and receive monthly average updates. For full rules, and information about how to join the RPI program, visit www.poolandbilliard.com/player.

Object of the game: "99" is played with nine object balls (one through nine) and a cue ball. Play is divided into nine innings with a maximum score in each rack of 11 points, and a maximum game score of 99 points. Like 9-Ball, the game is played in rotation, and the first ball contacted by the cue ball must be the lowest-numbered ball on the table. If players pocket any ball on a legal shot, they continue their inning until a miss, a foul, or completing the inning with a run-out.

Racking the balls: In each inning, the balls are racked with the nine ball in the center and the "inning ball" at the top of the diamond on the foot spot. The inning ball corresponds to the inning that is being played. Thus, in the first inning the one ball is the head ball, in the second inning the two ball is the head ball, and so forth. In the ninth rack, when the nine ball must become the top ball, the one ball is placed in the center of the rack. All of the other balls are racked in random order. On the break, the player is not required to contact the lowest ball first since the head ball is not always the lowest ball.

Beginning play: In each inning, the player begins with ball-in-hand behind the head string to break. After the break, the player begins with ball-in-hand anywhere on the table and continues until failing to legally pocket a ball, pocketing all of the balls, or legally pocketing the nine ball at any point. If the nine ball is made on the break, or legally out of order at any time during play, the player is awarded nine (ball count) points.

Keeping score: Beginning with the first inning, enter your break bonus (2 points if you made any balls on the break, unless you scratched) and your "ball count" score (the total number of balls pocketed in the inning, including balls made on the break). The sum of your break bonus (2 or 0) plus balls pocketed (1 to 9) will equal your score for the inning (maximum 11). In subsequent innings, add your new inning score to the running total.

INSURANCE BALLS

Insurance balls are balls that can be easily pocketed from many positions on the table. In 8-Ball, you save these balls as "insurance" for times when you may need to play risky position with the cue ball. If you don't get your optimal result, the insurance ball allows you to continue your run.

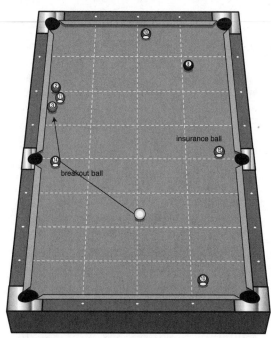

Figure 7.9 You can break up this cluster, knowing you've got the fifteen ball in the side as an insurance ball.

Figure 7.9 illustrates a typical insurance ball situation. You want to use the fourteen ball to break the eleven ball out of the pack, down the rail. If you hit the cue ball with center ball and medium speed, you can expect to hit the three ball full and move the eleven ball out along its two ball tangent line away from the rail. It may move to a position where you will take it next in your run-out, but if that doesn't happen, it's okay. The fifteen ball is insurance that you have another shot to put you back on track.

Your dilemma in figure 7.10 is that your two ball is tied up with the eleven. You could go for the break-out now by pocketing the seven in the corner, but you would have to do something risky such as cheating the pocket or spinning the cue ball to hit the two. The better option is to take the one ball, moving into a better position to use the seven to break out the two. Figure 7.11 shows you how. Cut the seven in the corner with a firm center ball hit. By hitting the two ball full, you move the eleven ball away from the pocket toward the thirteen, while the two rebounds from the rail to a more centered position. Hit this firm enough so that the cue ball moves toward the center of the table and the two ball clears. This leaves you with a shot on the five, your insurance ball.

TEAR OUT TRICKS

The middle game will present you with plenty of tricky situations that require you to clear pockets, move balls to a more advantageous position on the table, or break balls out of clusters. In 8-Ball, this is commonly referred to as "tearing out" balls.

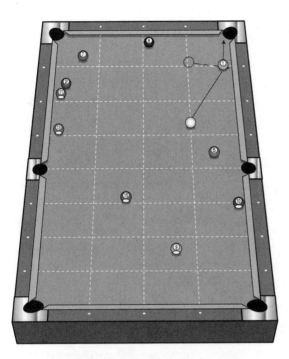

Figure 7.10 Your two ball is tied up with the eleven ball. Rather than taking a risky shot, use the seven to break out the two.

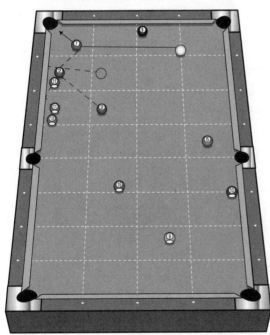

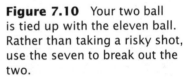

Figure 7.11 By cutting the seven in the corner, you're left with a shot on your insurance ball, the five.

In figure 7.12, your opponent has locked up the corner pocket with the eight ball and tied up your ten ball in the process. To clear the pocket, you must make the nine ball off the eight ball. There are two ways to play it. Let's begin with the best way—by hitting the nine ball into the rail first

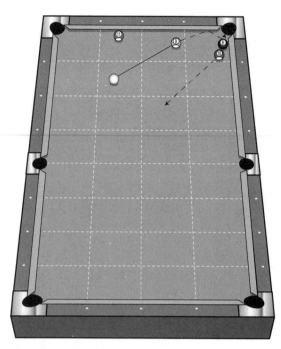

Figure 7.12 Breaking up a cluster with a well-played carom shot.

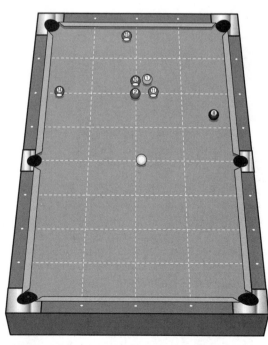

Figure 7.13 Tearing out balls after pocketing a ball.

(as shown in the figure). This accomplishes the following objectives: The eight ball will hit the ten ball more fully, forcing the ten to travel a greater distance. Because the eight ball hits the ten full, the eight will stay near the contact point. With a fuller hit on the nine ball, it's easier to keep the cue ball near the end rail to have a shot on the eleven.

The other choice you have is to hit the nine ball directly into the eight for the carom into the pocket, but this choice has its disadvantages. First, if you cut the nine ball more, you have less ability to stop the cue ball after contact. Next, if you cut the eight ball into the rail, its contact on the ten ball will be less direct and may cause one of the following results: The ten ball may not clear well enough. Because of your need to stop the cue ball, you may have to sacrifice speed, resulting in a poor break-out. The eight ball may come off the long rail toward the short rail and interfere with your shot on the eleven. All things considered, the rail-first carom is the safer shot.

Tearing out balls doesn't have to be accomplished with high-speed blasts. Speed control is the greater consideration. In figure 7.13, you have an opportunity to break up this cluster when you pocket the eleven ball in the upper right corner pocket. All you need to do is nudge the balls a bit to get a shot on the ten ball. But, if this shot is hit too hard, you run the risk of hitting the one ball to the rail, taking away one of the corner pockets for your fifteen. Figure 7.14 shows the outcome when the shot is hit with the right speed.

Tear outs can also be accomplished with safe shots. You may choose this option because an insurance shot is not available or because moving into the appropriate part of the cluster is too difficult to do indirectly. In figure 7.15, your poor position on the one ball makes it difficult to get any kind of angle to tear out the three ball. Instead, play the one in the corner and roll up for a safe shot on the three. Now you can more precisely hold that cue ball on the three, guaranteeing that the three stays positioned between the cue ball and the eleven, while the eight blocks a clear shot at the thirteen ball. Note: When two cluster balls are frozen together, you want to come into the shot with as full a hit as you can for a safe shot. This allows the most energy to be transferred from the cue ball to the second object ball. You can then accurately predict where the first ball and cue ball will go—that is, they will stay put!

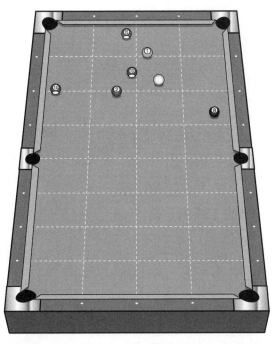

Figure 7.14 This shows the result of pocketing the eleven ball and breaking up the other three clustered balls.

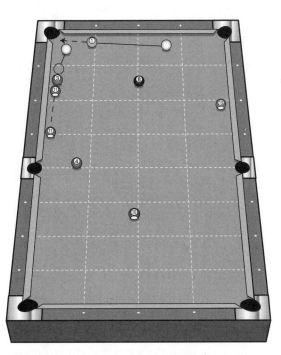

Figure 7.15 Playing position for a safety that will break up a potential problem cluster.

BALL-IN-HAND

Many of today's rules allow you to take ball-in-hand when your opponent commits a foul. These opportunities are golden, so make the most of them. In general, when you have ball-in-hand, you want to do one of four things:

1. Break up clusters.
2. Address trouble balls.
3. Plan and execute the optimal run-out.
4. Progress to a win through a three-foul situation (when allowed).

Clusters

In figure 7.16, your opponent scratched. You have lots of trouble to address, so you need to be patient and work one issue at a time. Consider the two possible shots illustrated. Either shot—when executed well—will break up two clusters and hide the cue ball. But which one is the best option? In shot A, when you shoot the thirteen into the twelve ball and hide the cue ball behind the nine, the best shot you leave your opponent is a two-rail kick at the eight. In shot B, when you shoot the fourteen into the twelve ball and hide the cue ball behind the fifteen, your opponent has the option of a much easier *one-rail* kick to make a legal hit on the eight. Shot A is the better choice.

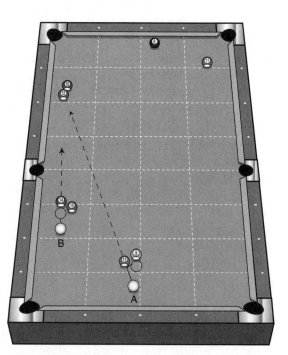

Figure 7.16 Shot A is the better choice for a cluster break up here.

Trouble Balls

Figure 7.17 illustrates a situation where you are again fortunate enough to have ball-in-hand. You don't have any clusters to worry about, but you do have a two ball blocked from its nearest pocket possibility by a stripe. You can consider clearing the pocket or breaking it out with a shot on either the one or the five, but there's an easier solution. Place the cue ball between the two ball and the long rail and shoot the two in either the left top corner or the left side pocket as shown. Once this ball is off the table, the rest of the run-out is a piece of cake.

In figure 7.18, you don't have enough room to place the cue ball behind the thirteen to shoot it directly into a pocket, but you do have another option. The five ball in front of the side pocket affords you a nifty little carom. Aim the thirteen into the left side of the five (as you look at it from behind the cue ball) and it will rebound into the side pocket. It won't take much speed to pocket the ball, so hit the shot firm enough to keep a proper stroke, but with cue ball position in mind. Use a center ball hit and be sure not to leave the cue ball frozen on the rail for your next shot, the eleven.

Plan a Run-Out

Obviously, if you get ball-in-hand and the table looks good, you'll be planning how to run the table. Even better than your first shot after the break in the opening of the game, ball-in-hand in the middle game offers the opportunity to address trouble spots first, and then proceed through the run. You'll have a greater variety of options, knowing you can start with the cue ball anywhere on the table.

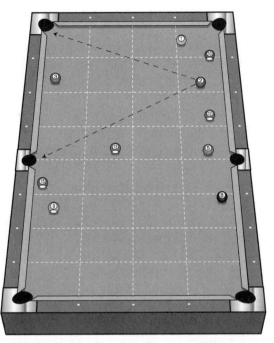

Figure 7.17 Ball-in-hand can allow you to address trouble balls with the most advantageous cue ball placement.

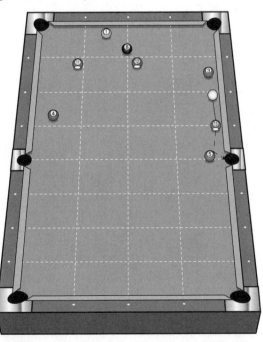

Figure 7.18 You can't get past the five to make this shot in the corner, so use the five ball to carom it in instead.

Play the Three-Foul Card

On the other hand, if the table doesn't look good, and trouble spots can't be easily addressed, you can plan a three-foul situation (when allowed) to win the game. (In most of today's 8- and 9-Ball game rules, three consecutive fouls by the same player constitutes loss of game.) Ideally, you will address at least one of your own trouble spots while playing safe with ball-in-hand. This way, even if your opponent makes a brilliant hit and your three-foul plan backfires, you'll have less mess to contend with.

MID-GAME SAFETY PLAYS

Just as in the opening game, the middle game will present plenty of safety opportunities. Even when a ball is available to pocket, your best shot might still be a safe play. Evaluate the risk and reward in each circumstance before making any decisions. For example, say your opponent has made the fatal mistake of running all of her balls and missing the eight ball. You, on the other hand, have all of your balls left. While this may strike fear in the hearts of many players, don't worry. You are in the driver's seat.

In figure 7.19, though you do have a shot on either the three or the four, with the cue ball so close to the end rail and the game on the line, both shots are very risky. Instead, take advantage of all the blocker balls on the table, while at the same time putting a little distance between the six and seven. This way, you make progress in positioning your object balls, and you have a high probability of getting back to the table, likely with ball-in-hand.

The resulting safety play shown in figure 7.19 illustrates a soft stun shot on the seven ball. The object ball moves up table toward the side pocket, while the cue ball drifts behind the six. You need only control the cue ball in this shot since it has three balls potentially blocking its path to your opponent's eight ball—the six, seven, and three. Even if the incoming player can see the left edge of the eight ball, the

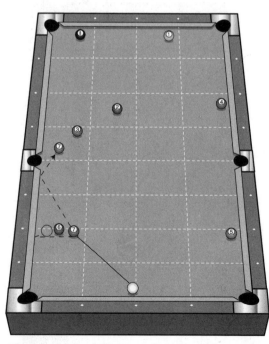

Figure 7.19 A clever safety play allows you to come back to an easier run-out.

distance between the cue ball and eight limits the player's shot choices and increases your chances of coming back to the table with a run-out opportunity.

In the situation shown in figure 7.20, a well-played safety can absolutely turn the game around. You have no incoming shot to pocket a solid, and you have the two and three balls tied up to boot. Cut the one ball to the left to place it in front of the upper left corner pocket. The cue ball will rebound off the short rail into the two-three cluster to open the trouble spot. Be sure to hit the far side of the two ball for the best results. In fact, you can even hit the rail first and come into the two. Using two or more available blocking balls side by side to create a "wall" is a strategic move that surfaces more often than you might think. Each additional ball available for this wall allows your shot a greater margin for error, translating into a greater chance for success.

In figure 7.21, your opponent has missed the one ball but tied up your eleven in the process. You don't have a good opening shot, but the beauty is that you don't really need one. It's more advantageous to play safe. One of your options is to cut the ten ball into the short rail so that it hangs near the corner pocket. This will make it easier to get to the ten ball

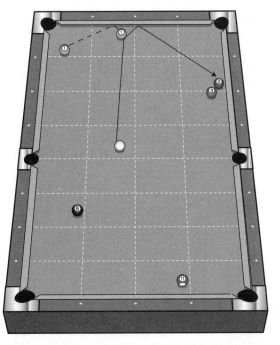

Figure 7.20 Hiding the cue ball behind one or more balls is a common safety in 8-Ball where more balls are in play.

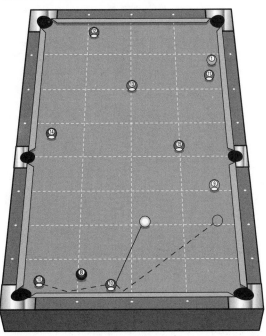

Figure 7.21 Playing safe in this situation allows you to position your group of balls in a more favorable position for your next turn at the table.

when you *do* run out. You've also blocked the corner pocket so that the eight ball can't go in there. The cue ball will come around near the long rail behind the nine, making it difficult for your opponent to even be able to kick at the one. If your opponent does make a good hit on the one ball, there's still a very good chance he will open up the eleven ball for you.

In summary, the middle game allows us to dust off those top-shelf shots, polish up our safety strategies, and get creative with our offensive play. If we've kept our head in the opening game, the middle game will represent the bulk of the execution of our plans. But it's also a way to come back from those bleak situations left you by an equally creative opponent. In each case, think of your cue ball as a finely tuned vehicle, ready to move in and around obstacles to get you safely back on course.

End Game Excellence

8

The end game is what you've had in mind from the very beginning. But sometimes, things don't go as planned. The 8-Ball end game is optimally about pocketing the last few balls for a win. Yet, if the plan goes awry, you will need something to pull out of your hat. Taking free shots, tying up your opponent, and blocking the pockets are proven favorites that will add plenty of notches to your match win belt.

TAKE THE FREE SHOT

The best things in life are free. In 8-Ball, the *free shot* is a term used to describe a low-percentage shot that carries little if any downside if it is missed. For example, figure 8.1 shows an opportunity to take a free shot at the ten ball on a risky length-of-the-table bank. If you make it, great! Your follow-up shot is an easy shot in the corner. If you miss, no problem. You hook the cue ball behind the eight ball, leaving your opponent a difficult kick shot. An added bonus is that if you hit the ten ball with the correct speed, you can leave it hanging in the corner pocket, taking that pocket out of play for your opponent's one ball.

Hit the cue ball full in the face just below center to stop it, with enough speed to get the ten ball to the other end of the table. If you overcut the shot a little, the ten may go long rail, then short rail, and end up blocking the one ball without hanging in the pocket. This way, even if the cue ball sneaks out from behind the eight, there's still no pocket for the one. Since it's more important to keep your opponent from seeing the one than it is to block the pocket or make the ball, your focus should be on cue ball control.

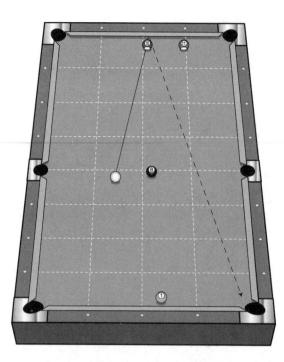

Figure 8.1 Take a free shot on the ten—if you make it, great; if not, your opponent still has no shot on his remaining object ball.

TIE UP YOUR OPPONENT

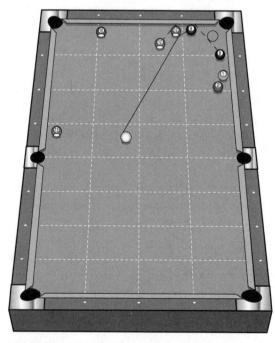

Another successful end game strategy is one that ties up your opponent's balls, forcing your opponent to do something creative, and therefore risky. This is particularly effective when you are playing someone who lacks imagination. Figure 8.2 illustrates an end game situation where you have no easy out for your stripes. The eight ball is blocking the pocket for the twelve ball. Neither the bank on the thirteen nor the tough cut on the ten seems to have a future. In this situation, you can advance your cause by breaking out the twelve and blocking the corner for use by the solids. Hit the twelve ball thin to get a solid carom on the eight.

Figure 8.2 Hitting the twelve ball thin allows a solid carom on the eight ball to block the corner pocket.

BLOCK A POCKET

In the end game, your options dry up as more and more balls are removed from the table. There are fewer safety options as well as fewer balls to pocket. Sometimes you're forced to take a difficult shot, so it pays to make the best of it. In figure 8.3, you came up a little short on the three ball, and this has left you with a difficult cut in the corner pocket. What you can do here to improve your chances of winning is to aim on the correct side of the pocket, so that if you miss, the three ball will block the pocket. Aim to undercut the three ball should you miss on this shot. This offers you a good chance of catching that outside pocket. With the proper speed it will fall in or

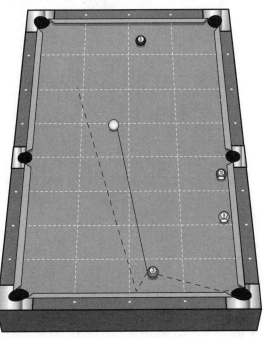

Figure 8.3 If you miss the three to the short side of the pocket, you'll still be able to block the pocket for your opponent.

hang in the target area, creating an obstacle for your opponent. If you overcut it instead, the three ball will rebound out toward the short rail, clearing the way for the nine and ten. Note that the cue ball travels to the other side of the table where you can end up with a shot on the eight if the three ball falls.

RETHINK YOUR OPTIONS

Sometimes you're faced with a decision whether to take an easy shot with tough position or a tough shot with easy position. In such a case, you need to do a probability assessment of the options. This assessment uses what you know about your skills and applies it to the situation at hand to calculate the best option. Typically, it will address actions in sequence or combination. Remember from your old math classes that the probability of two things occurring together is equal to the product (multiply) of the two things happening independently.

In figure 8.4, you ended up with an incorrect angle on the six ball. You wanted an angle coming toward the eight ball, but the cue ball rolled a little too far. You're now faced with an important decision. The cut in the side is easy, but moving the cue ball through all that traffic to get back on the eight is very risky. Let's say you can make the six ball in the side pocket 100 percent of the time but can only find the two-rail position 10 percent of the time. Your combined

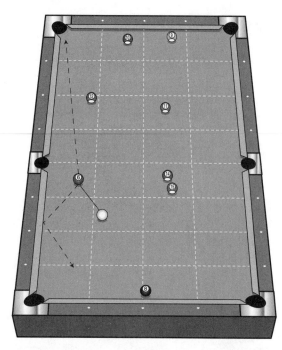

Figure 8.4 Cutting the six down to the corner pocket is the winning percentage play.

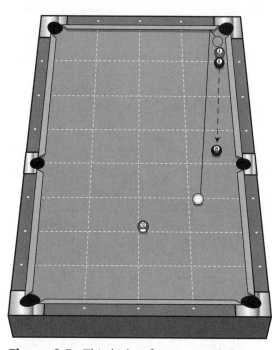

Figure 8.5 This kick safety accomplishes several objectives and leaves your opponent with nowhere to go.

probability for a successful shot is only 10 percent (1.0×0.1).

Your other option is cutting the six in the corner with straight draw to get position on the eight for the win. The shot is tougher, and you can only make it 60 percent of the time, but the position is easier and you can accomplish that 90 percent of the time. Your combined success probability in this scenario is 54 percent (0.6×0.9). Your chances to win are *much* better (more than five times) when you take the tough shot.

KICK SHOTS

Often in an end game situation, you will not have a clear shot at your ball but may be able to see an edge of it. Don't be afraid to look beyond a direct hit when this situation arises. In figure 8.5, your opponent has left your four ball tied up with the eight ball near the top right corner. You can see the edge of the four, but the best shot is a one-rail kick shot that will leave your opponent safe. Hit the cue ball with high right english into the short rail so that it rebounds fully into the four. This will loosen the eight ball from the four, pushing the eight toward the side pocket. The follow will serve to stop the cue ball once it contacts the four off the rail, effectively placing the four between the cue ball and the twelve. Recall that topspin becomes bottom spin when the cue ball rebounds directly from a cushion.

Three-Foul Rules

Just like the roll-out, another rule that players can take advantage of is the three-foul rule. Three consecutive fouls by the same player results in loss of game.

Three-foul options most often come into play when your opponent has already fouled once and given you ball-in-hand. Obviously, if you have an open run at the table, you'll go for it. But having ball-in-hand gives you no guarantee of a run-out. If you have two or three clusters in your way, even with ball-in-hand you won't be able to tackle them all. It's usually wise in this case, especially with your opponent already on one foul, to play another safety. If your opponent fouls again, you've got him on two fouls and can go for the three-foul win. (Note: In pro competition, you are required to tell your opponent that he is on two fouls in order to have the third foul count as a loss of game.)

Trying to defeat your opponent on the three-foul rule is often easiest just after the break. With most or all of the balls still on the table, it should be pretty easy to play an excellent safety and cause your opponent to foul again. Now your opponent is on two fouls, you've got him under pressure, and you've still got plenty of places to hide the cue ball.

A final word of caution: Have a plan in place. You should anticipate your opponent's response to your first safety, so you'll already know where you want to play safe on your next shot to hide the cue ball again. Nevertheless, you also need to remain flexible. Players attempting a kick tend to change the lay of the table, especially with poorly attempted kicks.

FINAL SAFETY PLAYS

The end game will still provide many opportunities for clever, game-saving safeties. In fact, it's the end game where they may become most important, as the strategic end game safe will likely determine the last shot of the game. In figure 8.6, each player has run down to the last ball. Since your opponent had no pocket available for her last ball, she rolled her eleven ball into your one ball to tie it up. Your best response here is a soft two-rail kick. With the one ball off the rail, it makes it an easier safety to complete, since you can either push the one to the rail *or*

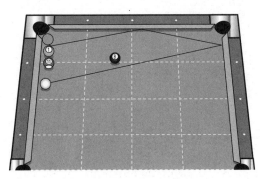

Figure 8.6 End game safeties like the shot illustrated require creativity and patience.

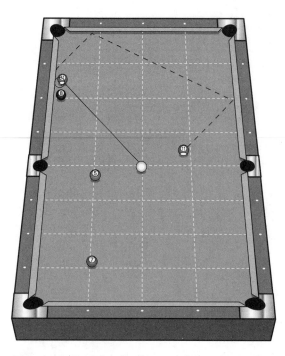

Figure 8.7 A bank shot, as shown here, is a high-risk shot, but the safety play offers a much better opportunity to come back to the table for a win.

push the cue ball to the rail after contact. As you line this up, keep two things in mind. First, speed is critical. You want to leave the cue ball on the rail behind the one if at all possible. If this is shot too hard, the balls will separate, giving your opponent some kind of shot on her eleven. Next, you want to hit the one ball as thin as possible for two reasons. A thicker hit will almost guarantee a scratch, and it will put more distance between the one and eleven. If you maintain the eleven's relative position to the eight ball, the eight ball takes away the possibility of both the one-rail and the two-rail kick shot for your opponent. She is really forced to come up with something show-stopping. If you fail to hit the one ball, it's not the end of the game. Your opponent still has her eleven ball tied up and has to find her way out of that situation. You will still get another turn at the table, though likely you'll again be returning *her* safety.

Whenever you can stop the cue ball behind a blocker ball and have an opportunity to freeze the two together, you have a very promising future. This will come up in end game situations, as shown in figure 8.7. Your opponent has missed the five ball, but your eleven is tied up behind the eight. You may be thinking you have two options. You can bank the eleven cross-corner, coming out one rail for the game-winning shot on the eight, or you can play safe. The bank shot is a high-risk shot, so let's examine what safety options are available. Hit the eleven ball full using a low center ball hit on the cue ball to stop the cue ball behind the eight. Your opponent will be lucky to find a two-rail kick from there. This is a shot where you must control the cue ball. Where the eleven ball lands is also important. You want to put it in the center of the table for two reasons. First, this ensures that it is not tied up with another ball. But just as important, leaving the eleven close to the center makes it difficult for your opponent to find a place for the cue ball where you won't have a subsequent shot at it. This of course is providing he can make a good hit on one of his object balls.

Figure 8.8 shows a situation where you could work the rack and go for the breakout on the eight-nine cluster. You'll have an insurance ball (the fifteen in the side), but there's no rule that says you have to pocket a ball. Why not let your opponent try to break out the eight-nine cluster? Or, rules permitting, let your opponent three foul in the process. Take a soft half-ball hit on the ten ball, moving the cue ball to the long rail on the same side of the table as the eight. The diagram illustrates the optimal outcome. When a blocking ball is left close to the cue ball, it often takes away the tracks for one- and two-rail kicks. Keep this in mind when visualizing the final position of the balls.

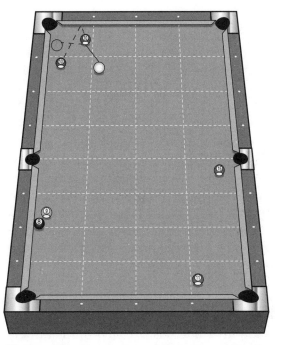

Figure 8.8 Here's an end-game example of letting the other player make the mistake. Let your opponent try to break out this cluster.

TEAM DYNAMICS

Knowing yourself and your opponent is the first step in preparing for effective competition. However, if you are playing on a team, it is just the first step. A team must work together as one body. Not only must each part function well independently, but all parts must also work in coordination with each other.

First, you must understand what a team is and what it is not. A team is a group of people working together in a coordinated effort. It is not a bunch of people doing their own thing. It is not one person carrying the load of the world on his shoulders. It is not one person putting on a show. As Phil Jackson is fond of saying, "There is no 'I' in *team*."

Here's what some experts say about enhancing team cohesiveness:

• **Open communication is essential.** This includes communication among the players as well as between the players and the captain. Communication is a group process, and mutual trust and respect are essential in order to keep the channels open.

- **Team building starts with self-awareness and the individual's relationship with the team.** Each player needs to take a real look inside to understand his own strengths and weaknesses, and he must communicate them to the team. Maybe you really play well under pressure. Maybe you don't. Your team or team captain needs to know that, not only to create the most strategically advantageous position for the team, but also to give *you* a high comfort level. You cannot play your best if you are uncomfortable.

- **A good team has a well-defined philosophy.** The philosophy and values you define will lay the groundwork for all subsequent interactions. Your team philosophy must be developed by the team as a whole in order for it to have any meaning. If the philosophy exists before a team member joins, the new member must understand and be in agreement with the values prior to becoming part of the team. Team values may include punctuality, good sportsmanship, sobriety, and honesty. A team philosophy may define expectations such as the following: Each player is expected to arrive on time and ready to play. Each player is expected to pay league fees each night he or she plays. Each player is expected to exhibit good sportsmanship, which includes playing fair and honest, showing respect and courtesy to the opponent, and providing a supportive and positive environment for team members.

- **Set goals.** Develop pride and a sense of collective identity within the group by setting realistic team and individual goals. Feelings of pride and satisfaction develop when individuals and groups attain challenging but realistic goals. *Group and Organization Studies* published results of a field experiment on cadet squadrons at the U.S. Air Force Academy. The results mirrored plenty of studies done in the area of teamwork, and showed that cooperative activities for groups, such as goal setting, are likely to elevate training and competitive performance standards. When performance expectations are higher, higher performance follows.

Your team should focus on process goals rather than outcome goals. Outcome goals look at end results (such as winning a tournament) while process goals look at processes (such as being relaxed and focused when stroking the ball). When you perfect the process, the outcome is unavoidably successful. Process goals can vary from keeping your head still on every shot, to making a ball on the break, to not taking a flier when a good safety is available. Your teammates can help keep you on track when they know your goals.

- **Develop a team identity.** Some sport psychology experts recommend developing a team song, motto, or routine to facilitate team identity. It doesn't have to be anything fancy. It can be as simple as engaging in a victory toast and chanting your team's name at the end of the evening's play. One way to facilitate team identity is to get everyone involved in determining the team name or team shirt design. The trick is to move the players away from playing for themselves and move them toward playing for someone or something else. Psychology and leadership experts call these external sources of motivation *personal objects.* The players find something outside of themselves to be identified with. Leadership experts know the value of creating a "greater good" to which their followers will dedicate themselves. This is the level where players can expect to play "out of their head."

- **Stay positive.** Nothing can bring the whole team down quicker than a negative attitude! On the other hand, if you want to be a winner and a leader, you must set the emotional agenda, rather than follow it. When things start to go wrong, take a clear position that you are going to instigate a turnaround. Refuse to be sucked into the air of negativity. Radiate a belief that you *will* turn things around. When you build such an air of contagious certainty about you that things will be different, your teammates will catch it!

In reflecting on the night's performance, focus on successes before discussing any failures. A positive group climate is developed if the positive nature of group and individual performance is highlighted before errors and omissions are discussed. Remember, whether a shot is made or missed, each one is a learning experience.

- **Have fun.** We've covered this territory many times before, but it is never as important as it is in team play. Resolve to enjoy the game and the social activity regardless of the outcome.

Team play can be one of the most rewarding experiences of your pool life—or it can be one of the most painful! Avoid the heartbreak and disappointment that comes with poor team dynamics by using these proven team-building strategies.

Top-Notch 9-Ball

9-Ball is today's fast-paced pro game, the game you'll see played on television and at 90 percent of professional events. Yet few aspiring players know the real ins and outs of 9-Ball as it's played by the best players in the world. Part 3 is broken into three chapters.

In chapter 9, "9-Ball Openers," we talk about the all-important beginning of every 9-Ball game. That includes skills and strategies needed for racking the balls and knowing what kind of a rack your opponent is giving you. Once the balls are neatly racked, it's time to mess them up with the perfect break. While the game of 9-Ball has traditionally called for a power break, you'll learn why more and more professionals are adjusting their games to employ a softer break shot. Finally, we'll talk about the first shot after the break, including information about when to go for a run-out, play safe, or exercise your push-out option.

In chapter 10, "Winning Moves," we'll get into the meat and potatoes of the 9-Ball game, all that happens after the game's opening shots. You'll learn how offense and defense are used equally to win games, and you'll learn game-winning tips used by today's top players.

The final chapter, "Table-Closing Tactics," delves into new territory, with illustrations and discussions of those end game situations that can be so intimidating to even the most experienced player. You'll use many of these types of shots throughout a game of 9-Ball, but they become really critical in the end game. As you'll soon learn, whether playing an offensive or defensive shot, 9-Ball end game strategies require the ultimate in patience and creativity.

9-Ball Openers

Rack 'Em! Oh, how pool players love to say those words, and how they hate to hear those words spoken to them. Unless they're playing under alternate break rules (more common in today's pro arena, but rare in the amateur sector), the player who wins the game then breaks the next game. The player who lost the game racks the balls.

As the racking player, it's your responsibility to provide as tight a rack as possible for your opponent, meaning all the balls in the rack will be "frozen" or touching each other. This isn't always easy. Divots in the cloth, worn or dirty cloth, and worn or dirty balls will challenge your racking ability. Nevertheless, you're on your honor to provide the best rack possible. (In pro events, players may in fact request a rerack if they are not satisfied with the rack given them by their opponent.)

RACKING STRATEGY

While it's considered a cheap shot to "put a rack" on an opponent (give him a bad rack), this doesn't mean you can't employ racking strategy. Strategically racking the balls simply means to put them in positions within the rack to make a run-out as challenging as possible for the breaking player. If your opponent knows racking strategy (and you should always assume that he does), he'll surely be placing the balls in the rack in the most advantageous position too, so there's no guilt in this type of action as the racking player.

Typically, the most difficult types of run-outs in 9-Ball are those that force you to move the cue ball up and down the table. Therefore, it would make sense to place the balls in the rack in a way that makes traveling long distances

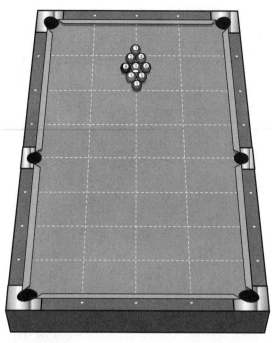

Figure 9.1   The ideal 9-Ball racking order.

more likely for your opponent. Referring to figure 9.1, you'll notice that the balls are racked with the requisite one ball in front, followed by the three and five balls just behind, then the six, nine, and eight, then the two and four, and the seven at the back.

When a player breaks the balls, the back three balls of the rack will tend to head down table, while the other balls move up table, toward the head spot. Now, look at figure 9.2 to see a sample break result using this configuration. As you can see, the player must shoot the one up table, come back for the two, head back up for the three, then down again for the four—you get the picture. As previously discussed in the chapter on pattern play, more distance means more chances your opponent can make a position play mistake, putting you back at the table.

Now, taking this idea one step further, if your opponent is breaking from one side or the other, you can take further advantage of your racking strategy. If the incoming player is breaking from the right-hand side of the table, you'll want to place the three ball (still in the row of two balls behind the one) to the right side of the rack and place the two ball (still in the bottom row of two balls) also to the right side. This sends the two ball down table toward the center of the short rail and keeps the three ball close to the one ball on the other side of the table, again, making maneuvering between the one, two, and three more difficult.

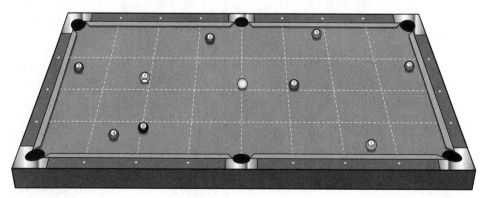

Figure 9.2   Example of how balls might look after breaking an ideal 9-Ball rack.

The Danger Signs

Every player is entitled to check the rack being offered by the opponent, on every rack in a match. This is fully expected at the professional level, and pros can request that the racking player rerack the balls until they are satisfied the rack looks good enough to break. This doesn't mean you have to take this rule to extremes. Plenty of players do provide the best racks they can for their opponent as a matter of courtesy. Continuing to check their racking throughout a match, when they have provided you with nothing but perfect racks, can be insulting and make you look like the poor sport.

When professionals check an opponent's rack, here's what they look for (see figure 9.3):

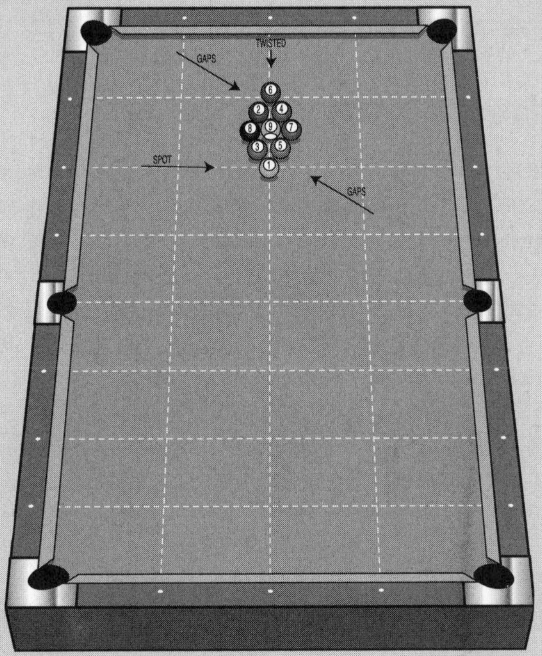

Figure 9.3   This rack is not ideal.

- **A twisted rack.** A twisted rack occurs when the one ball, nine ball, and back ball in the rack don't align perfectly with the center diamonds on both short rails. Twisting or tilting the rack one direction or the other makes it tougher to pocket a ball on the break, and tougher to control the cue ball after impact.

- **Space between balls.** A perfect 9-Ball rack means every ball in the rack is touching every ball next to it (to the best of the racking player's ability). If there is space between the balls, the cue ball will not have as much impact on the pack, as energy will be transferred to the one ball but not as much to the balls behind the one. Space between any of the front balls is a definite sign of a slug rack. Space between the bottom three balls (those closest to the foot rail), however, may actually allow the nine ball to escape the rack more easily and head for the corner pocket.

- **Missing the spot.** The one ball should be centered on the foot spot, which is marked by a thin paper or fabric decal on most tables. If the one is in front of the spot, it is more difficult to pocket a ball on the

> break. Note that professional rules only require the base of the one ball to be touching any part of the foot spot. Players can (and do) take advantage of this by racking as far forward as possible, while still keeping the base of the one ball at the front edge of the spot.
>
> If you've checked the racks, found them satisfactory, and you're still struggling with your break results, either you're breaking badly, or you're the victim of bad racking. The easiest way to combat a bad rack is to slow your break down. Taking speed off the break on a bad rack can easily counteract its effects. The balls will still spread apart, and you'll have a better chance of pocketing a ball and continuing your turn at the table. Many players have adopted the softer break in their games as a matter of course, as you'll soon find out!

Check Your Rack

Some players believe the only way to win is to give their opponent a bad rack (often referred to as a *dead*, *stiff*, or *slug* rack). We don't condone this sort of poor sportsmanship, and neither should you, but as it's often said, the best offense is a good defense. Knowing what to look for in poor racking, and knowing how to minimize the effects it will have on your break, is your best defense.

When you execute a firm, crisp break shot, it should be accompanied by a firm, crisp sound as the cue ball smacks into the rack of balls, sending them scattering around the table surface. A poorly racked pack of nine balls will result in a noise that's more like a thud than a crack. This is your first clue.

Other effects of breaking a bad rack include no balls going past the side pocket and lots of clustered balls. This happens because the rack was manipulated in such a way as to avoid the full impact of the cue ball on the entire rack.

Changing With the Times

As pool evolves, so does its equipment, and the rack is no exception. Racks offering perfectly frozen balls, such as those that you've probably seen used in many televised pro events, have changed the way players rack, and break. Lou Sardo, inventor of the Sardo Tight Rack™, discovered in early testing of the product that providing a perfect rack every time virtually guaranteed that one of the back balls would sail directly into one of the corner pockets. As you might imagine, while eliminating the nastiness associated with getting a bad rack from an opponent bent on skulduggery, it also made for too much predictability in the game. When the women's pro tour decided to use this rack on a regular basis, they sought to alleviate this problem by moving the rack of nine balls forward, so that the nine ball was placed on the spot, rather than the one ball.

Of course, whenever a change such as this occurs, professional players immediately begin to practice with the new position and the new equipment to find their most advantageous strategy for both racking and breaking. In the

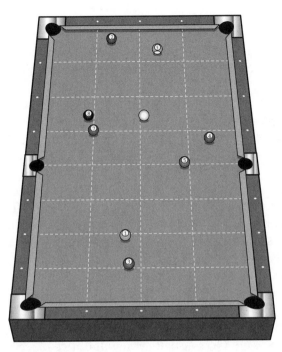

Figure 9.4   Result of a rack after a soft break.

case of the Sardo rack, a move toward softer breaks was the result (with the goal of pocketing the one ball in the side and parking the cue ball near the center of the table).

This naturally led to a change in racking strategy, and the most predominant element we've witnessed is to place the two ball (again, still in the back two-ball row) on the *opposite* side from which the player is breaking. Figure 9.4 shows how a rack that this strategy was used for might look after the break. Since the break is hit softer, the cue ball will usually land in the vicinity indicated. If the one is not pocketed, it will be near the side or drift down table, as shown. Now, look where the two ball lands—the most predictable of the bunch. It will nearly always come to rest near the center of the short rail, with enough balls between it and the one ball or cue ball to make getting back to the two a difficult proposition.

BREAKING DEVELOPMENTS

The first secret to a good 9-Ball break is realizing how important it is to the game. Too many players take this shot for granted, thinking it's simply a way to spread the balls apart so both players can continue shooting. This attitude usually results in players trying to hit the balls as hard as they can, without regard for accuracy.

In 9-Ball, more than in any other game, the break, if executed with the same loving care as any critical shot, can determine who controls the remainder of the game. If you are the breaking player, and you spread the balls nicely but don't make a ball, you must expect that your opponent can run nine balls. If you pocket three balls on the break but can't see the one ball, you're faced with a kick or a roll-out, which lets the other player back to the table, where anything can happen. At the professional level, the break becomes *the* most important shot, because the player who breaks, pockets balls on the break, and has a shot on the lowest-numbered ball on the table is a percentage favorite to win the game. If you've had the opportunity to witness the pros live or on television, you've no doubt heard players comment that they won (or lost) because their break was working (or not).

Pick a Side

Old-timers may hearken back to a time when breaking from the center was the preferred spot for a 9-Ball power break. But with evolving rules of the game that made 9-Ball progressively more offensive, players began to closely study which break areas offered the best chance of pocketing balls to continue a run. While there's less distance between the cue ball and the one ball when breaking from the center, and while it's certainly your best opportunity to get a solid hit on the one ball, statistics still heavily favor breaking from just a few inches inside the side rail.

Now, which side is best for you? Many right-handed players may feel more comfortable beginning on the right-hand side of the table, and left-handed players on the left-hand side. However, where you should break from is better dictated by your stroke. A right-handed player may have a tendency to put left-hand english on the ball, and vice versa. In this case, you're better off breaking from the opposite side of the table, since the english you naturally place on the cue ball will help stop or "kill" it after impact.

Once you've developed your power break from your "favorite" side, it will pay to be adept at the other side as well. Occasionally you will notice players switch sides based on what the table is telling them. If, for instance, your opponent is consistently pocketing balls by breaking from the left side of the table, while your break from the right-hand side is proving fruitless, you'll want to be able to easily adapt.

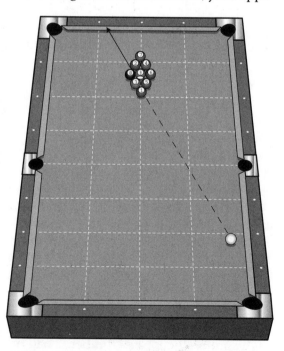

Aim True

Once you've picked your favorite side, you'll need to pick the spot you want the cue ball to arrive at the one ball to best impact the rack. There's no negotiation here; the best result will come from the most solid hit. Figure 9.5 shows both the ideal spot to aim the cue ball and the area of the rack (behind the one) on which to focus your visualization. By aiming through the one ball to the balls in line

Figure 9.5 Aim through the one ball on the break, straight through the imaginary line pictured.

Johnny Archer and Max Eberle lag for the break. The player whose cue ball comes back closest to the rail chooses who will break the balls.

behind it, you'll be assured the most solid hit into the rack. This will also help you to focus on your follow-through.

Now to return to those natural tendencies in your stroke. If you naturally put a touch of left english on the cue ball during your follow-through (and most players don't hit absolutely dead center because of their individual stroke crossovers, dominant eyes, stance, and so forth), you will want to address the cue ball with a little low right english. This serves to straighten the cue ball's path to the one ball, offering the most power, and the most control over the cue ball after impact.

Adjust Your Body

A power 9-Ball break requires minor adjustments in your physical approach because you must direct substantially more force into the shot. Many of these adjustments will occur naturally to you but are worth describing here so that you can spot trouble areas quickly.

1. Stand up a bit more on the break shot. This will give you more room to swing the cue and make it easier to put your entire body into the shot.

2. Your weight is distributed equally in a normal stance, offering a solid base from which to execute most shots. On a power break, however, the majority of your weight can be on the leg that's closest to the table. This puts you in the best position to allow your body to propel the cue forward through the shot. Watch the top players on television and you'll see that their back leg leaves the ground as they come through the shot, putting all their weight on the front leg (see figure 9.6).

3. In normal, everyday shots, your cue stick will head down toward the cloth in your follow-through. On the break shot, however, the best players begin

by aiming low on the cue ball, and the cue stick comes up in the follow-through as the elbow drops and the body moves forward. Again, this offers maximum power.

4. Keep the grip loose. Tightening the grip tightens the arm and wrist. It's easy to assume that you would want to "strong arm" this shot, but you'll achieve higher speeds and more power from an arm and wrist that are swinging relaxed and loose.

Accuracy Versus Power

While you can't predict where all the balls will land on the break, you can keep the cue ball close to the center of the table, which will increase your chances of having a shot at the next ball. This

Figure 9.6 Tony "the Tiger" Ellin was a famed player known for his powerful break shot.

requires a below center hit on the cue ball, propelling it squarely into the one ball.

Since you want as solid a hit as possible on the one ball, it pays to work on accuracy first, and then build up your power. Begin by breaking at the speed of a medium hit shot to make sure you're hitting the one at the right spot. Then slowly build up your speed until you can achieve a powerful yet controlled result.

Today's top players are learning the value of the softer break. You may be surprised that a soft break still manages to drive balls toward pockets, and it allows the best control of the cue ball. However, keep in mind that the rules of 9-Ball dictate that at least four balls must contact a cushion after the break. Failure to do so will result in ball-in-hand for your opponent. Experiment with less power in your break to see how it affects the shot, especially if you've been breaking at top speeds.

THE ROLL-OUT OPTION

The first shot after the break in 9-Ball offers an option not available during the remainder of the game. This option is referred to as a *roll-out* or *push*, and it can be used one of two ways. If you are the breaking player, and you pocketed balls but cannot see the lowest-numbered ball on the table, you may elect to send your cue ball to a different position on the table without contacting the lowest-numbered ball. Your opponent then has the option of telling you to shoot again or taking the resulting shot herself. If your opponent broke and made nothing on the break, and you come to the table only to find you can't see the ball you need to shoot at, you may exercise the same option.

The roll-out rule in 9-Ball was implemented because the first shot after the break was the one shot in which both players could be unjustly penalized. For example, the player breaking the balls pockets nothing on the break, but the opponent cannot possibly hit the lowest-numbered ball on the table. The breaking player shouldn't be unfairly rewarded for a poor break. At the same time, the breaking player could pocket two balls and everything's looking rosy, when suddenly the cue ball is kissed to a point on the table where the player cannot hit her designated object ball.

Do I Need a Break Cue?

Break cues and jump cues have become popular options for players. At least half of today's top players make use of a break cue, for a variety of reasons. First, a break cue can keep your normal playing cue in better shape, as you're bound to more quickly flatten out a leather cue tip on power shots (along with other stress factors). Second, a break cue offers options you won't need in your regular cue. A break cue can be built to specifications that make it ideal for breaking, such as the following:

1. It can be simpler in design and more durable than a regular cue. For instance, many players, even if they normally play with a wood cue, will use a break cue made of graphite or some other composite material, believing there is more action to be had from these materials (not unlike trends in golf and tennis).

2. It can feature a slightly larger tip (one-quarter to one-half millimeter). This provides more control since more of the cue tip's surface contacts the cue ball.

3. It can be a different weight than your normal playing cue. Some pros swear by heavier cues, but the trend now is toward lighter break cues. While the heavier cue offers more weight behind the shot, the lighter cue allows more speed.

Sounds like a good rule, and it is, but only if you know how to take full advantage of the opportunity. The push shot can be a useful tactic to set up a shot that you're more capable of executing than your opponent. It can be used to change the lay of the table. It can be used to set up a safety. All these tactics require a plan. Without one, you're just bumping the cue ball to a place where you (and your opponent) can see the object ball, and it's likely your opponent will take the shot, and the game, while leaving you to wonder where you went wrong. Likewise, if your opponent elects to roll out, you better be anticipating what she might intend to do, especially if you can do it first!

Serving Up a Push

Choosing to roll out is a difficult decision. You're intentionally giving up the table to your opponent, hoping he will pass a shot back to you, or hoping he will fall into your well-planned trap. When you do choose to roll out, there are a variety of options you can exercise. Knowing each option available will give you more choices when faced with handing the table over to your opponent.

Change the Table

This is a popular roll-out option among pros and amateurs alike. By changing what could be an "easy out" on the table, you improve the likelihood that your opponent will not run out and that you will get another "at bat." One way to

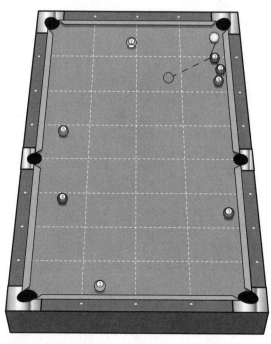

change the table is to make a mess of the balls by creating clusters on an otherwise open table. In figure 9.7, you've done this by shooting the two ball just in front of the four. You can still see the one if you're required to shoot again, but it's a long, tough shot. Meanwhile, the two and four are tied up, and even if your opponent chooses to shoot, he'll have to work his way out of the mess, or play safe. If he tells you to shoot again, you can play safe yourself by sending the one ball around the table and behind the mess you've created.

Or, let's say you've executed a nearly perfect break, but the nine has rolled perilously close to a pocket, and you can't see

Figure 9.7 One good roll-out option is to change the lay of the balls, making a run-out more difficult for your opponent.

the one ball, as shown in figure 9.8. You can't take the chance of kicking at the one ball, because even if you get a good hit, you're likely to set up an easy one-nine combination for your opponent. Time to change the table. Pocket the nine, stopping the cue ball so you can hit the one ball if required to shoot again. You leave a tough shot to get back on the two, and the pocketed nine ball is returned to the foot spot on the table.

If you don't have an opportunity to create a cluster or pocket a ball to change the table, you can also consider making a run-out more difficult by sending an object ball to a poor position, such as near the rail on the opposite side of the table, or on the rail

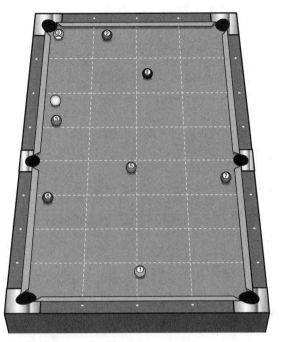

Figure 9.8 By pocketing the nine on a roll-out, you avoid giving your opponent a combination shot.

adjacent to the side pocket. Your goal is to make the table less advantageous for a run-out, so it pays to be creative. Think what your opponent would do in the situation, then outsmart him by thinking a few moves ahead.

Set Up Your Favorite Shot

If you can't see the lowest-numbered ball on the table, but you don't want to leave a shot your opponent can make, consider your top-shelf shot options, especially if you know your opponent has a weakness in one of these areas. If you have a natural affinity for banking balls, for example, roll out to a bank. Are you amazing at kick shots or kick safeties? Hide your opponent and let her decide if she wants to risk the kick or send it back to you. If jump shots are your thing, and you want to be in a better spot to stun the crowd with a jump shot, by all means, do so. Your opponent will be forced to try the same shot (which she may be uncomfortable with) or send it back your way. Since these are typically low-percentage shots, make sure you really have the advantage before making such a decision.

This tip can work in reverse as well. If you know your opponent loves to play banks, for instance, but only pockets 1 in 10 of her attempts, by all means set up a bank shot. She'll fall into your trap, unable to resist the temptation of what may be her favorite shot, only to miss, or lose control of the cue ball for the next shot.

The Tempting Long Shot

Perhaps the most common roll-out is to increase the distance between the cue ball and object ball, leaving a long, but makeable shot. If you can leave a straight-in shot, do so. Typically, your opponent will be so grateful to see the ball that he'll take a flier at the tough shot, often returning you immediately to the table. If you've left a straight-in shot, even if your opponent makes the ball, his chances of getting to an advantageous position for the next shot have been greatly reduced. It's surprising how easily players fall into this trap. We refer to it as shooting at a shot with no future. It doesn't matter if the shot can be made if you can't go any further.

Returning the Serve

Don't assume you're the only one who knows these push-out tricks of the trade. Your opponent may know them too (and may even have read them here!). It's equally important to know how to return a push that's been served to you, or handed back to you, as it is to know how to execute one in the first place.

A good roll-out is like a well-executed chess play. It involves strategy, predictions of what your opponent might do, and alternative plans should your opponent do the unexpected. If your opponent rolls out to a certain area of the table, you have several quick decisions to make:

1. What is he up to?
2. Does he have the ability to execute the shot he left for himself?
3. Can he execute it with any degree of efficiency and proceed through the rack?

If the answer to the third question is yes, you'll obviously want to take the shot yourself, rather than watch him run out. If you don't have confidence in your ability to make the shot left to you, play safe. Again, you're playing the percentages, and this means playing a tight game that forces the other player to make the mistakes that will return you to the table.

You know how to plan your own roll-out to a long, straight-in shot, and your opponent may leave you in the same predicament. Don't make the mistake of thinking this is your favorite shot and jump up to shoot, only to find yourself in no position to continue your run.

In this situation, you have two options. Let your opponent go for the shot and fall into his own trap, or think up a creative safety. If you assume your opponent has a safety plan in mind, you're better off playing the safety. In the example shown in figure 9.9, you've been left with a long, straight-in one ball. If you make the shot, you'll probably even have a shot at the two ball, but the rest of the rack is looking precarious. Instead, execute the safety shown by hitting the side of the one ball, and let your opponent deal with a tougher table in the process.

If your opponent has left a tough but makeable shot, you may be able to take a calculated risk and pocket the ball, so long as you plan ahead. Play the shot so that if you miss, you'll still have an opportunity to return to the table. This is a free shot—also called an *either/or* shot—it's great if you make the shot, but if you miss, you won't "sell out" the rack to your opponent. This is especially useful if your opponent has rolled out to a favorite shot of his own. You may not be as adept at the shot, but by calculating where your cue ball will end up, you can still make the attempt and take the chance away from the other player.

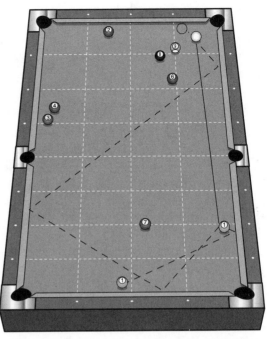

Figure 9.9 Exercise a safety option and let your opponent make the mistake of trying to tackle a tough rack.

Don't assume too much and hand an easy shot back to your opponent. No matter the lay of the table, you can use a safety to increase your chance to return to the table as quickly as possible. It's easy to plan ahead to play safe if you've rolled out and the shot is handed back to you, and it's easy to play safe with what your opponent has left you, especially if you can see the object ball. Shooting at a roll-out option with a defensive move is usually the best strategy. It puts the other player back on the defense to kick at the ball (and leave you a shot), break up a cluster, or even give you ball-in-hand.

The Last Word

While the mental key to executing and returning strategic push shots is thinking ahead and being creative, the physical key is speed control. Without it, you could put yourself in a more precarious situation than that which first led you to rolling out. You could roll the cue ball too far and not be able to see the object ball, whereupon your opponent will enjoy watching you kick at your own unintended safety. You could wisely pocket a hanging nine ball, only to find that again you can't see the lowest-numbered ball. Your opponent will tell you to shoot again. You could roll out to a near perfect bank opportunity, only to find you've left yourself a bit too much angle to get to the next ball.

As with any other shot, the roll-out deserves its fair share of practice. Each time you break the balls in practice and have no shot on the one ball, play a push, and then pretend you are your own opponent and decide your next move. Like practicing safeties, it's more of a challenge to predict the outcome, but knowing your options and staying in control of this shot will keep you at the table.

The opening of any 9-Ball game begins with proper etiquette (providing a good rack), and continues with a carefully executed break that will, in the best of scenarios, offer a run-out opportunity. The first shot after the break will either be the beginning of your offensive strategy (a run-out) or a defensive shot (safety or roll-out). Practicing your options, especially in regards to safeties and clever roll outs, will offer you more control at the table, whether you are the breaking or incoming player.

10

Winning Moves

Unlike the game of 8-Ball, where you'll always have a distinct beginning, middle, and end game, 9-Ball is divided less equally. A game of 9-Ball is divided into the opening moves discussed in the previous chapter, and, for lack of a better term, the rest of the game. The nine ball can be made any time during this "rest of the game" phase, so winning moves could well happen before all the balls have been cleared from the table. Because the balls are shot in rotation, you must use slightly different tactical maneuvers than those available to you in other games. There are fewer offensive options. You'll always be shooting to hit the lowest-numbered ball on the table. Period. 9-Ball can be infuriatingly predictable, say some. 9-Ball can depend totally on luck, say others.

Nevertheless, it's the game played in the majority of regional tour and local cash tournaments, and the game most often played at the professional level. Lucky or not, top players manage to diminish the luck factor and defeat their opponents with skillful regularity. Predictable or not, players seldom run many consecutive racks in competition. Offense and defense are on equal terms, as are mental and physical skills. Often the winning edge will come down to not only what you can do, but also to what you know.

KNOW WHEN TO HOLD 'EM

To play winning 9-Ball is to run perfect racks with surgical precision, and equally, to know when that's not possible and opt to play a brilliant safety that will ensure your quick return to the table. Giving up the table doesn't have to mean giving up control. The pros may make it look easy on the tube, but there's more to this game than meets the eye. Once you get past the opening break and decide whether to shoot or roll out, a number of new options will present themselves. For them to present themselves thoroughly, you must be paying attention. Remember that the keys to winning 9-Ball include having patience, understanding options, controlling your speed, and knowing when to play it safe.

Be Patient

Just because the game looks fast and plays fast doesn't mean you won't need to take your time in the beginning of the rack. Watch the pros on TV and note that it's those shots just after the break that demand the most time and patience from the player at the table. Here's what they're deciding, and the thoughts behind those decisions:

1. **Can I run out from here?** If the rack is wide open (and many racks are), you'll be looking to see if you can accomplish a run-out. You know that the best way to run a rack is to keep cue ball movement to a minimum. Therefore, part of deciding whether the rack is indeed "wide open" is determining the ease with which you can get from the lowest-numbered ball left on the table to the next ball in the rack, and so on, right up through the nine ball. The more you play, the less time this evaluation will take.

2. **What is the key shot in the game?** As you decide on your run-out pattern, one shot will usually stand out as the "key shot" in the rack. This key shot refers to a shot that must be accomplished to near perfection in order to complete a run-out. For example, in figure 10.1, it looks rather easy to get from the one ball to the three ball, and then over to the four ball, where a simple stop shot will get you on the five. But, when pocketing the five, if you aren't careful to land on the proper side of the six, your trip to the seven, eight, and nine will be difficult. In this case, the five ball is the key shot, the one you'll need to take some extra care toward, the shot that can make or break this rack.

3. **If I can't run out, when can I play the best safety?** Let's say you've broken the balls and pocketed the three ball, but the rack ended up looking like the example in figure 10.2. The

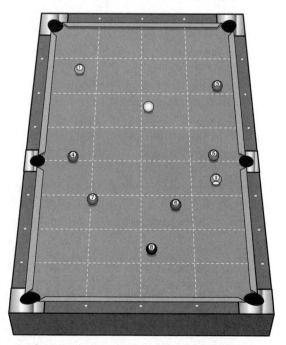

Figure 10.1 Look for your key ball when planning a perfect run-out. In this rack, your key ball is the five ball.

six and the eight are a mess, especially with the lower-numbered ball being closer to the pocket. Yes, this is one of those times when giving up control of the table will actually work in your favor. It's called letting the other player make the mistakes, and it's a key strategy in 9-Ball.

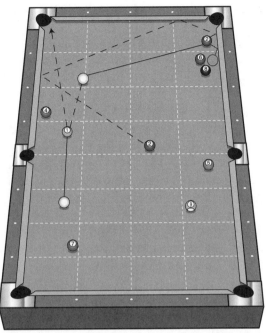

Figure 10.2 In this rack, you want to find the best safety option.

Now that you've decided the rack is not suitable for a game-winning run, your next decision is when to play safe. While it may seem smart to immediately play safe on the one ball and leave plenty of balls on the table for your opponent to sort through, a better option exists. In this example, the one is in fact easier to pocket than to send to a safe place. And if you pocket the one (with the intention of rolling up for the two ball), you can play an excellent safety on the two, sending it to one end of the table, while tucking the cue ball neatly in that six-eight cluster. If you're lucky, you'll even nudge the cluster enough to break out the six so you can achieve a run when you get back to the table. And yes, with this safety, you're sure to get back to the table. Even if the two is hit legally, the chances of it being pocketed anywhere are slim to none.

Top-ranked player Karen Corr is known for her patience at the table.

Understand Your Options

Naturally, once the game is in full swing, if a player loses control of the table, a whole new series of options will present themselves. And, while professional 9-Ball games may only last an average of one or two innings, most games will offer more. This means that despite a player's best efforts to accomplish a run, he misses a ball midway through the rack and allows the other player back to the table. Or, a player misses position and is forced to play safe, again letting his opponent back for a shot.

At this point, the same options as described in the previous section will apply, with a few new twists. You may be looking at a nasty safety your opponent left you, in which case you'll have to

1. kick at the ball to get a legal hit,
2. attempt to pocket the ball with your kick,
3. kick safe, or
4. commit an intentional foul.

On the other hand, you may have a shot, but it may require use of a top-shelf shot such as a bank or curve shot. Or your opponent may have fouled and you have ball-in-hand. In this case, you'll need to decide if that ball-in-hand allows you to run out from there, or if you can play another safe that may lead you to a three-foul win. Let's take a look at how some of these options may present themselves.

In figure 10.3, your opponent has left you without a direct shot, but the two ball is very close to the corner pocket. In this case, you'll want to not only get a good hit, but also pocket the ball and go for the subsequent win. This is a kick that comes up often in 9-Ball. Play it a bit long, so that even if the cue ball contacts the short rail first, you will still pocket the two ball. (It's advantageous to be able to pocket kick shots this way, as it allows more position options for the cue ball and reduces the chance of scratching.)

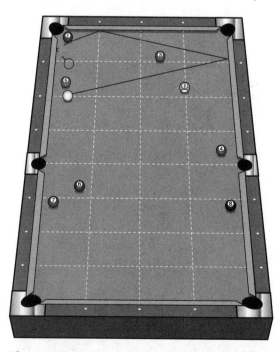

Figure 10.3 Executing an offensive kick shot can get you out of this rack and into the winner's circle.

Figure 10.4 shows an excellent way to get a legal hit while still leaving your opponent in poor position. (This is a fantastic shot that Vivian Villarreal performed in a match against Allison Fisher.) By executing a soft-kick safety, Vivian got the hit and left another tough shot, eventually resulting in her gaining control of the table.

Figure 10.5 shows a good intentional foul opportunity. You have little chance of getting a good hit on the one ball, and your opponent will no doubt get ball-in-hand. In this case, it's better to take an intentional foul by creating a cluster for your opponent and letting her battle the table layout, even with her ball-in-hand advantage. By softly hitting the five into the seven ball, you will make a mess of the five, seven, and four balls. This will prevent a run by the incoming player.

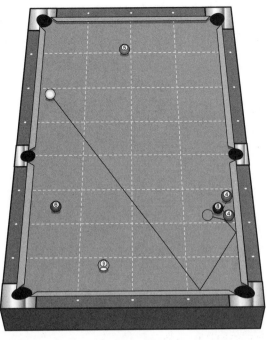

Figure 10.4 Get the hit and still leave your opponent safe. This legal hit is a real crowd pleaser.

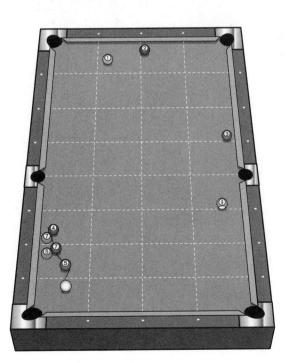

Figure 10.5 Sometimes it's best to take an intentional foul, especially when you can leave a real mess for your opponent.

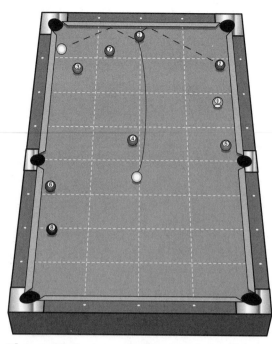

Figure 10.6 A top-shelf curve shot will get you out of a tough spot in this rack.

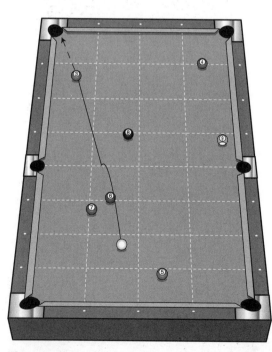

Figure 10.7 Getting a hit on the three will require "taking to the air" with a well-executed jump shot.

Top-Shelf Shots

9-Ball is the perfect game in which to hone your top-shelf shot skills. Again, because you're required to contact the lowest-numbered ball on the table first, you'll have opportunities for curve and jump shots, banks and kicks, and lots of caroms and combinations!

In figure 10.6, your opponent has missed and left you somewhat safe. You can perhaps see the very left edge of the two ball, and it's a risky kick with other balls nearby. Using your curve shot skills will allow you to get the hit. The cue ball will head left, the two ball will head right, and you'll leave a tough shot for your opponent.

In figure 10.7, you've been left with an ideal situation in which to pull out your jump cue. You can't see the three ball, and a kick is difficult due to interfering balls. The ball interfering with your direct hit into the three is far enough away from the cue ball to make a full-ball jump possible. Finally, the three is close enough to the pocket that a good hit is liable to make the ball.

Figure 10.8 shows a bank shot opportunity that comes up quite often in 9-Ball. The six ball can't be cut into the side because the angle is much too sharp. But a cross-side bank not only pockets the six, but, with a bit of follow, sends the cue ball to a good position for a shot on the seven ball.

Since the rules of 9-Ball dictate that you must hit the lowest-numbered ball on the table first, combination shots will be plentiful. You may not have a clear shot on the one ball, for example, but you may be able to send it into another ball lying in a pocket to make that ball and continue your run. Caroms are less obvious, but equally advantageous. Figure 10.9 illustrates a situation where you have no pocket for the two ball, but the nine ball lies near the pocket. Attempting a three ball combination in this situation would be a low-percentage shot, but you can successfully carom the cue ball off the two and into the nine ball.

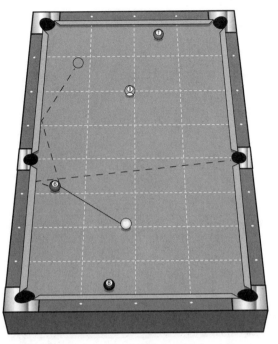

Figure 10.8 A cross-side bank shot allows you to continue the run.

Hanging Balls

Figure 10.10 illustrates two shots where your knowledge of how to pocket hanging balls will come into play. In shot A, you need to bring the cue ball back around the table for the nine. Players usually hit this shot with high right english, trying to send the cue ball to the bottom rail first on its way back to the nine. The english will grab and tend to kill the cue ball, forcing it to

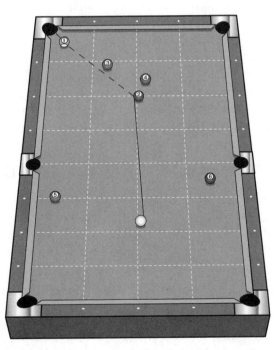

Figure 10.9 Caroming the cue ball off the two can result in a crowd-pleasing game win.

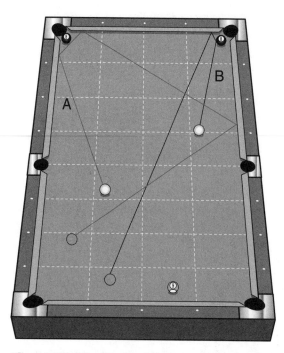

Figure 10.10 Don't underestimate the practice involved in getting perfect position off hanging shots. They come up often.

come up short for position on the nine. Instead, play the rail-first shot shown, which allows the cue ball a natural two-rail path after contact with the eight. You'll need to spend time practicing these shots to know how the cue ball reaction will vary with the thickness of the hit on the object ball.

Shot B offers another easily made ball, but don't underestimate the shot. Hitting this one too thick will again result in the cue ball coming up too short for a good shot on the nine. A thin hit (as illustrated) allows the cue ball to pocket the eight, clear the pocket edge, and contact the short rail. The cue ball retains most of its energy so it will travel easily back up table.

These types of shots are very easy to make but are often a problem for the player who does not control the cue ball after pocketing the ball. To practice, place balls at or near pockets all around the table, and work each one. Try to get your cue ball to a variety of positions, including the "safety valve" table center position.

CONTROL CUE BALL SPEED

While patience is the ultimate virtue needed for successful 9-Ball competition, speed control is the ultimate skill required. Because you always have only one ball that you must make contact with, poor speed control will result in poor position. Poor position on one shot can become worse on the next shot, and so on, and so on, until you're forced to give up control of the table with few balls left for your opponent to pocket.

Again, you have options for keeping your speed control on target and the cue ball from traveling too far. As you know, thickness of the hit isn't the only thing that will affect cue ball speed. Cue ball speed will also be determined by force of the shot, spin, and use of the rails.

Near and Far

While your ultimate goal is to attempt pinpoint position on every shot you pocket, it isn't always practical, nor possible, especially in 9-Ball. This is when knowledge of the right side and wrong side comes into play—knowing on which side of the next ball you'll need the cue ball to arrive to successfully continue a run.

This often comes down to the "near/far" principle. In figure 10.11, you're shooting at the three ball, and you want to get on the correct side of the four ball to easily move on to the five ball. (Remember, you should always think in groups of three!) As you decide on your path for the cue ball after pocketing the three, it becomes obvious that if you miss your exact desired position, you're still in a decent spot if you get to the shaded area. In this case, it's better to go "too far" than not far enough.

Conversely, in figure 10.12, if you go too far, you're sunk. In this case, you're better off coming up short on your position. The shot will be more difficult than your optimal position, but at least you'll still have a shot, and one that will get you to the next ball in the rack.

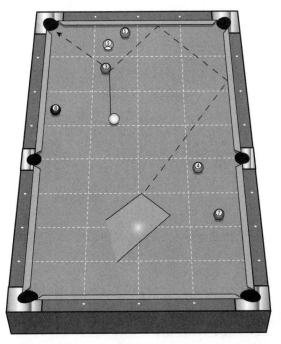

Figure 10.11 Getting to the correct side of the four ball to continue your run means it's better to go a little too far than not far enough.

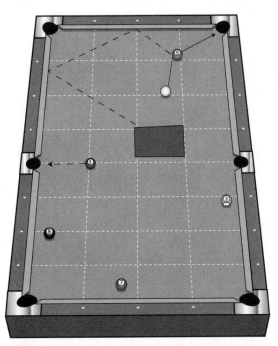

Figure 10.12 In this situation, use a softer touch since coming too far will put you on the wrong side.

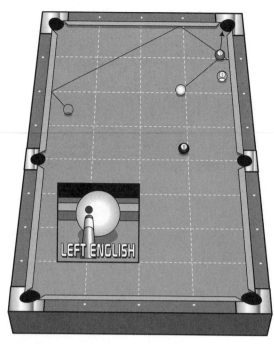

Figure 10.13 Inside spin offers you better position.

Spin to Win

You know that changing the spin on the cue ball, whether hitting it high, low, inside, or outside, will alter its path, and this will come in handy when you're knee-deep in 9-Ball pattern play. In the example shown in figure 10.13, a center ball hit on the cue ball when pocketing the seven ball would result in poor position for the eight and nine. But by using inside spin (in this case left english), you can send the cue ball three rails to be in perfect shape to make the eight ball, and then roll up gently for the nine ball.

Figure 10.14 illustrates a shot where outside spin will get you where you need to

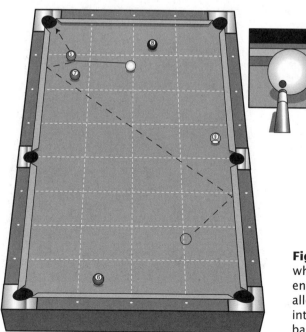

Figure 10.14 This shot, when executed with low-left english and a soft stroke, will allow you to gracefully avoid interference from the seven ball.

be. You need to get from the five ball back to the six ball. Straight draw would send the cue ball into the interfering seven ball. But using low outside english (in this case left english) allows you to weave the cue ball through the interference and back up table for the six. This shot requires a slow, controlled hit.

Follow and draw offer similar pattern play enhancing options. Figure 10.15 illustrates a shot on the one ball, that if hit with center ball, will rebound off the rail and head the opposite way of where you need to be for the two ball. The seven prevents you from traveling around the table back to the two. Likewise, you cannot draw the ball. But a firmly hit follow shot, commonly referred to as *force follow*, will allow you to pocket the one and drastically alter the path of the cue ball. The cue ball will hit the long rail and "grab," and this will spin it down the table for position on the two.

For the shot in figure 10.16, most players would use follow on the cue ball so after contact with the one it would drift toward the short rail for "short side" position on the two. There's a better shot, both for cue ball control and to avoid getting too close to any pocket (and a shot that still allows you to come into

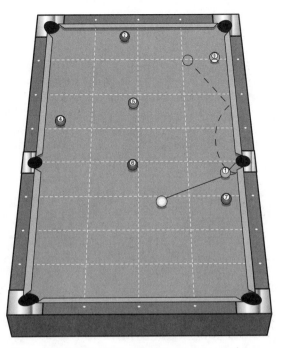

Figure 10.15 Enhance your pattern play here with a force follow stroke on the one ball.

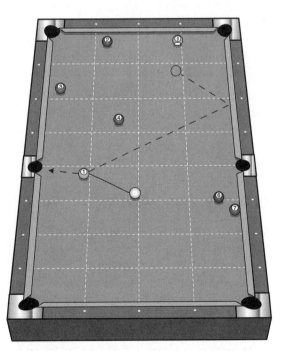

Figure 10.16 Drawing off the one ball allows easier (and better) position on the two ball.

Too Close for Comfort

When you're nearly down to the nine, you want the easiest shot possible for the win. That can cause you to get a bit too aggressive. You get too close to your work—too close for comfort. That's when a few tricks up your sleeve will produce the right shot that combines perfect aim with perfect cue ball control to still win the game.

In shot A in figure 10.17, you're using outside english to spin in the object ball. Aim to miss this ball since the outside english will push the cue ball into the nine sooner than you'd expect.

Conversely, in shot B at the right, inside english will push the cue ball away from the object ball, so you'll aim to hit this ball. But the inside spin allows the perfect hit to cleanly pocket the ball, without turning the cue ball loose around the table.

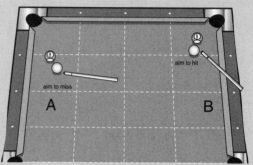

Figure 10.17 Careful aim, steady cue ball control, and proper use of english will consistently pocket these shots.

the angle of the two). Draw off the one ball with the intention of contacting the opposite long rail midway between the side and corner pockets. This allows you to get to the side of the two you'd prefer to be on (the two is closer to the pocket), rather than the short side shape (the two is farther from the pocket).

Using the Rails

Of all the speed control techniques for 9-Ball pattern play, none will come in more handy than taking advantage of the cushions bordering the table, more commonly referred to as *using the rails*, either long rail to short rail or vice versa. Many players are afraid to do so, perhaps because they cannot easily predict the path of the cue ball after contact. While this takes practice and may seem tough at first, you *must* learn how to do this to have an advanced 9-Ball game. The payoff is extraordinary.

Here's an example. In figure 10.18, you've ended up with a sharper angle on the eight ball than you'd like, which will make it tougher to get position

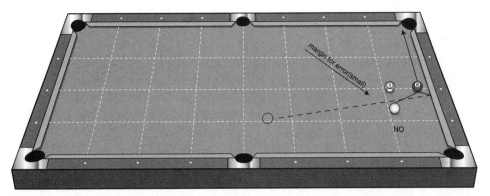

Figure 10.18 One-rail position doesn't provide the most ideal option.

on the nine ball at the same end of the table. You have to hit this ball hard enough to get it to the pocket, and hit it thin. This will send the cue ball much farther than you want it to go. Using one cushion position will result in a sharp-angle cut on the nine—never a high-percentage play on the game ball.

You can get a better result by using a second rail, as shown in figure 10.19. In this shot, you draw the cue ball off the eight ball, into the short rail, and then it contacts the second rail. The short rail also takes some speed off the ball. This leaves you with a better angle on the nine for the win.

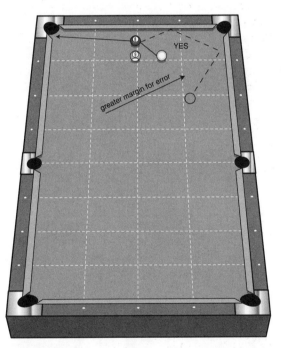

Figure 10.19 Using a second rail is the better option.

SAFETY PLAYS

As you've seen already in this chapter (and will see plenty more in chapter 11), defensive moves play as important a role in 9-Ball as offensive pattern plays. Whether you're left with a low-percentage shot or a low-percentage rack, the safety can turn things around.

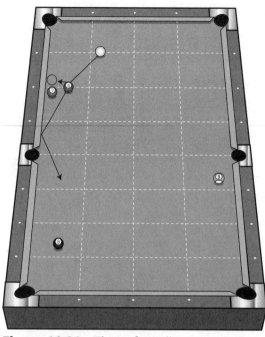

Figure 10.20 This safety allows you to hide the cue ball and let your opponent try to kick at it, likely leaving you a better run-out option.

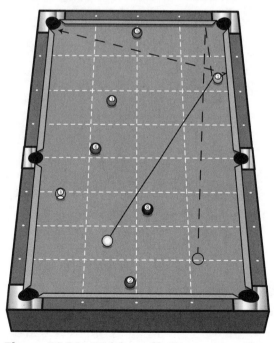

Figure 10.21 With lots of balls to run interference if you miss, banking the one ball and letting the cue ball come back up the table toward the two is an excellent free shot opportunity.

Figure 10.20 illustrates a low-percentage shot situation. True, you could attempt the six down the long rail, but it's a tough shot, with even tougher position options for the seven ball. Rather than attempt the improbable, opt for the practical safety. Send the six ball down table while killing the cue ball behind the seven, then let your opponent deal with the percentage play!

Figure 10.21 illustrates another safety that does double duty as a two-way shot. By banking the one cross-corner as shown, you've got a free shot to possibly pocket it and continue your run. But, whether or not you make the one, you will leave your opponent safe.

Two-way shots, often called *free shots*, are a 9-Ball favorite. They offer the comfort of a defensive move, with the bonus of a continued run or a win should the shot come off perfectly. Two-way shots are usually attempted with banks, combinations, or caroms.

Figure 10.22 illustrates another two-way shot safety. This one uses a combination. It's a tough combination, but that's fine since you can plant the cue ball behind the eight should the nine not find its mark. Remember, when attempting a free shot you must pay attention to where your cue ball will land. It's no good going for a tough shot if you don't make the ball and give your opponent an easy shot.

The game of 9-Ball gives you the chance to put into play all the concepts you've been working on throughout this book. Because 9-Ball is a rotation game, requiring you to have to contact one particular ball on the table first, you'll be consistently faced with opportunities to execute creative safeties, dazzling pattern plays, and amazing top-shelf shots. 9-Ball is popular for exactly this reason—it requires you to display every advanced skill in your arsenal in order to win games.

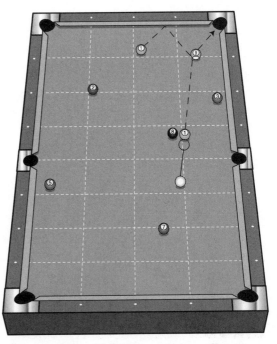

Figure 10.22 This two-way shot offers a combination. Make it and win the game; miss it and leave your opponent safe.

Table-Closing Tactics

Once a 9-Ball rack is played down to the last remaining ball and the nine ball, lots of maneuvering can occur. (Of course, this assumes the game isn't won with an earlier combination or carom.) In 8-Ball, there is a distinct end game because both players must pocket all of their balls before attempting the game ball. But in 9-Ball, that "end game" will only take place if the last ball or two remain and a safety battle ensues. Nevertheless, the questions most often asked by aspiring players revolve around those last two balls—how to play safe, how to return safes, and how to decide between offensive and defensive moves.

Each of the "final shots of the game" described in this chapter can become an entity unto itself—a game all its own, even. After all, in 9-Ball, you can run the entire rack, miss shape on the nine, and be forced to come up with a top-shelf shot or give up the table. Your opponent can run the rack and then play safe on the nine, in which case a top-shelf shot or a well-played safe could still bring home a victory for you.

Further, though these shots illustrate specific situations at the end of the game, each shot can and *will* come up, in many variations, throughout the rest of the rack. Therefore, knowing these end game specific strategies will also be of tremendous benefit to you during the rest of your 9-Ball pattern plays.

TWO'S A CROWD

If there's only a couple of object balls and the cue ball left on the table, one of the object balls will be the nine ball, and the other will be the lowest-numbered remaining ball. For the purposes of illustration, we will use the eight and nine ball, but of course it could be a lower-numbered ball (for example, the eight ball is pocketed earlier on the break or on a combination shot, and the seven is

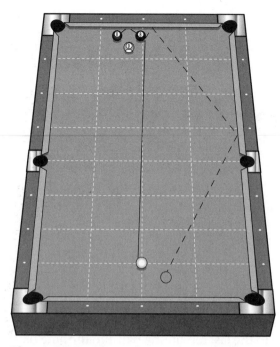

Figure 11.1   The end game is no time to lose patience. Return this safety with a safety.

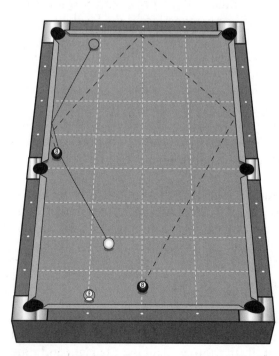

Figure 11.2   The eight is a risky shot—better to play safe.

the last ball left with the nine). With only two balls remaining on the table, safeties with blocking balls will naturally be more unlikely, while position play will be dictated by the exact position of the remaining balls. Bad leaves or safe leaves will require well-planned returns. The end of the 9-Ball game will test your skills, your creativity, and your patience!

In figure 11.1, the eight and the nine have been left at one end of the table, and the cue ball at the other end. As you'll note, there's no viable bank on the eight ball, since there's not enough room to hit it on its left side, and hitting it on the right side will only cause it to head into the nine. The smart play is to return the safety with a thin hit on the right side of the eight ball. This will allow the cue ball to head back toward its original position, while sticking the eight even closer behind the nine. You need to hit this ball very thin, so that the eight ball will travel only a short distance, and most of the energy will be left on the cue ball to return it to the other end of the table.

Even if you're left a shot on the eight ball, you may still be better off playing a strategic safety. In figure 11.2, you've been left an opportunity to make the eight, but you risk scratching in the side pocket. Even if you get lucky and miss the scratch, you will have less than ideal position to pocket the nine. Opt for the safety by sending the cue ball down to the short rail, and sending the eight ball around the table three rails to land in the center of the short rail on the other end.

In figure 11.3, the eight ball can't be hit directly, but you can kick rail first into the eight and still end up safe on this shot. If you use a follow stroke as indicated, the follow will reverse itself after contact with the cushion, and the cue ball will stick behind the nine ball after sending the eight ball to the other end of the table.

Though each of these "ball before the nine" safeties employs a slightly different methodology, they all have one thing in common—the

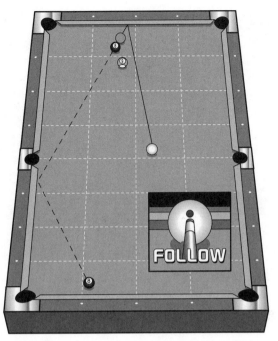

Figure 11.3 Kicking the rail first on this shot still allows you both a legal hit and a safe result.

use of distance to leave a tougher incoming shot for your opponent. In two of the three cases, you are also able to use the nine as an obstructing ball, your other weapon in the end game battle.

LAST CALL FOR A WIN

One of three things will happen when your opponent comes down to the final, game-winning nine ball:

1. Your opponent will make the nine and win the game.
2. Your opponent will miss the nine.
3. Your opponent will play safe on the nine.

Obviously, you will only return to the table in the latter two cases. The question is, if you get back to the table on the nine (and it happens often), what will you do?

Pick Your Spot

Naturally, if a shot presents itself, you'll go for the win. But remember, just like any other shot in the game, you'll want to first pick a destination for the

Figure 11.4 Multi-titled 9-Ball champion Francisco Bustamante uses careful planning to make the game look easy.

cue ball. You should pretend you have another shot after the nine that you need to play position for. Believe it or not, the number one reason players miss makeable nine ball shots is because they don't take that extra second to pick a destination for the cue ball. Not doing so prevents you from seeing the whole shot. You focus too much on the game ball without deciding where the cue ball is headed. This can result in poor follow-through or a punch stroke as you attempt to simply get the nine into the pocket. In other words, what you need to do is extend the thought process to include cue ball control, ensuring a full and well thought out approach to the game ball (figure 11.4).

In the example illustrated in figure 11.5, you're looking at a shot at the nine that can be easily made. By picking a destination for the cue ball for position

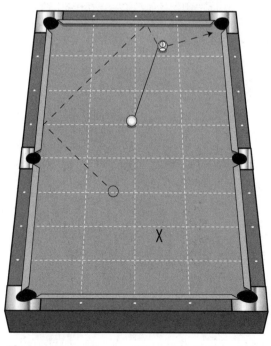

Figure 11.5 Play position with the cue ball on every single shot, even the nine ball.

on the imaginary X ball, you can focus on making the nine and sending the cue ball to a desired position on the table. This keeps you totally into the entire shot at hand, so you treat it with no less importance than any other shot in the game.

On this shot, you must also remember to play the nine ball with a below center to center ball hit on the cue ball if possible. You don't want to play position for an imaginary ball that requires you to place a lot of follow or english on the cue ball. The below center hit offers the most control, the most focused follow-through, and the least chance to make a cue ball control error.

Finally, we've chosen this particular shot to illustrate our point because it's a mistake we've seen made time and again, even by pros. Not having a destination for the cue ball in this example can easily result in a scratch in the side pocket. Again, you want to pick a spot that keeps you mindful of where the cue ball will travel. This will help you avoid the unnecessary pain of a well-struck shot that has a bad result due to poor planning.

No Shot on the Nine

A misleading headline, of course, because you'll always have a shot on the nine. It just might not be an easy shot. And it might not be an offensive shot. But there's always a shot. The fun comes in finding the one that will win the game for you. This is the area of 9-Ball strategy that really keeps you on your toes. Your opponent may leave you in a treacherous position that forces you to (a) take a tough, top-shelf shot for a crowd-pleasing win or (b) hand your opponent back a tough shot and hope he makes the error that will send you back for the applause.

If your opponent leaves you without a shot that can be easily pocketed, your options will range from long-distance shots to frozen ball shots, and from difficult offensive moves to calculated defensive moves.

Offensive Reactions to Distance

Let's first take a look at some offensive possibilities for when you face table layouts where the cue ball has been placed at or near one rail, and the nine ball on the opposite side of the table. Any offensive reaction will depend on the exact angle of the cue ball to the nine ball and the nine ball's proximity to the cushion.

In figure 11.6, the cue ball and nine ball have been left in such a way that a bank shot is possible, provided your top-shelf shot skills are up to par. A crisp enough hit is needed to ensure that the nine ball doesn't lag up and not quite reach the pocket. You want to stay as close to a center ball hit on the cue ball as possible—this shot is all about control. Mastering it will win you many games, and it's a real crowd pleaser, too!

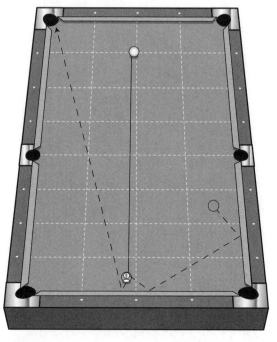

Figure 11.6 If your top-shelf bank shot is ready to play, this shot is a consistent game winner.

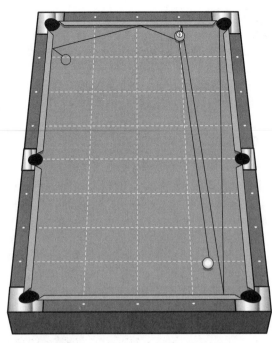

Figure 11.7 Hitting this ball crisp allows a double bank.

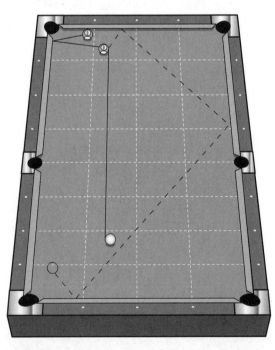

Figure 11.8 This long, thin cut can leave you safe if you aim to overcut the ball should you miss.

Here's another example of how a firm hit could be valuable. In figure 11.7, you've hit the bank shot a little bit short, but lucky for you, because you hit it crisp, the nine ball travels back down table for the win! Believe it or not, this shot comes up often during games, both with long rail and short rail banks.

Obviously, a bank shot isn't your only option. Figure 11.8 illustrates a leave where the nine is a little closer to the pocket. In this case, most players are better off with the long, thin cut. The bank angle is less natural, so the thin cut becomes the higher-percentage play. You want to hit this shot with just enough speed, so that if you miss the shot (to the long rail side of the pocket), the nine will come to rest on the short rail and leave your opponent safe again. This is one of those shots where visualizing the inside edge of the cue ball to the outside edge of the object ball is quite helpful. The danger in this shot could be in missing the object ball completely, so make sure you've practiced this shot before pulling it out in competition. (Missing the ball and awarding your opponent ball in hand has happened to plenty of pros, you are not immune, either!) It's also a shot where you need to have a definite destination in mind for the cue ball, otherwise the angle off the nine or any unwanted english may send the cue ball careening into a pocket.

Defensive Reactions to Distance

More likely in the long distance and no shot scenario is a defensive reaction that forces your opponent to "take the flier." However, you can't assume that a defensive move is any less difficult in this crucial part of the game. Controlling both the cue ball and the nine ball will be key to leaving your opponent in an unfavorable position. These shots will require just as much—if not more—practice than those offensive crowd pleasers.

Rail-to-rail safeties with no blocker ball options come in three basic flavors: the full-ball hit, the half-ball hit, and the thin hit. Figure 11.9 shows the full-ball hit safety, in which the goal is to double hit the object ball. The nine will bounce into the rail and back into the cue ball. Optimally, both balls will end up in a vertical line to the center of the table, forcing your opponent into a tough safe or an equally tough bank shot.

Figure 11.10 illustrates the half-ball hit. In this case, since the nine is so close to the rail, a thin hit would bounce the nine ball out closer to a makeable shot. But by executing a half-ball hit, you can leave the cue ball and nine each near the second diamond on opposite sides of the table.

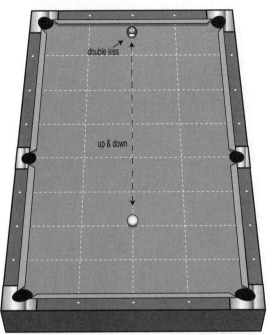

Figure 11.9 A tricky, but very effective, full-ball hit safety.

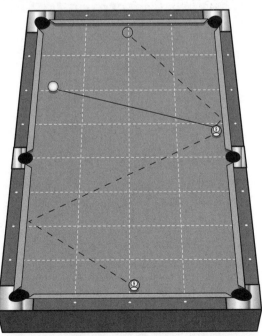

Figure 11.10 This half-ball hit safety sends the cue ball to the center of one short rail, and the nine ball to the other end of the table, leaving your opponent a low-percentage shot.

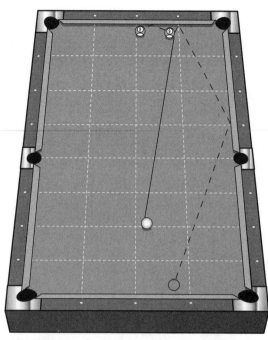

Figure 11.11 The most common safety on the nine ball when it is the only ball left on the table requires a thin hit as shown.

Figure 11.11 shows the most common safety (most common in part because it's the easiest to control). If you hit the nine ball as thinly as possible, it will move very little. At the same time, most of the energy will remain on the cue ball, sending it back down near its starting position. Practice this shot to get a feel for both the speed needed to bring the cue ball back and for how thin you can hit the object ball. Too thick, and the nine ball will travel too close to a pocket. Too thin, and you could miss the entire ball. That happens more than you might think, even in pro competition!

Offensive Reactions to Short Shots

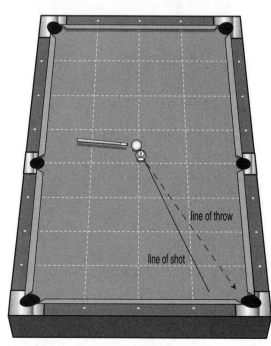

Figure 11.12 Offensive shot for this odd leave on the nine.

Often enough, it's your own mistake that will lead you to a tough final shot on the nine. You may pocket the eight, knowing you want to get just close enough to the nine ball for a game win, when lo and behold, you get way too close. Depending on the angle of the shot left, you may have a direct shot into a pocket, or a bank option.

In the situation shown in figure 11.12, you have played to get near the center of the table and have stuck yourself right to the nine ball. It doesn't look like you have a shot, but here's where some inside knowledge will produce a game win. This is called a *throw shot*. If you hit the cue ball on the opposite side of where most players assume they'd want to hit it, the cue ball will "throw" the object ball into the pocket. Slower speeds actually result in more throw on the object ball. This is a bit of a "feel" shot and well worth some practice time.

Figure 11.13 shows another shot where you got too close for comfort. In this case, the cue ball and the nine ball are not frozen together. A cut shot isn't an option, but a carefully planned bank shot is certainly possible. By hitting this with low, outside english, you can attempt the bank and still send the cue ball near the center of the short rail. Play this shot with enough speed that if the nine misses its mark, it will head to the center of the short rail opposite the cue ball.

Hint: On shots where there's little distance between the cue ball and object ball, keep your bridge hand close to the cue ball to offer more control. Then, remember to follow through, as even short shots require proper follow-through. Figure 11.14 illustrates a leave where there's more distance between the cue ball and object ball. A long bank is possible. You have the added luxury of being close enough to the object ball to aim it more easily than the long-distance bank. As you'll soon see, this leave will more often be approached with a defensive shot.

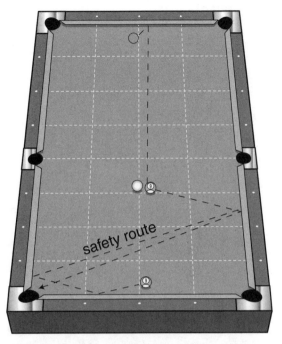

Figure 11.13 Low, outside english allows you to attempt the bank shot.

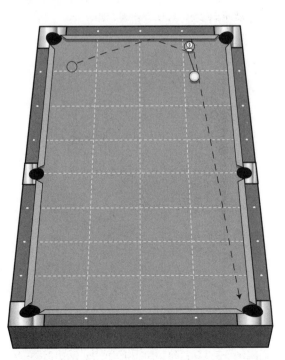

Figure 11.14 A difficult yet crowd-pleasing bank shot.

Defensive Reactions to Short Shots

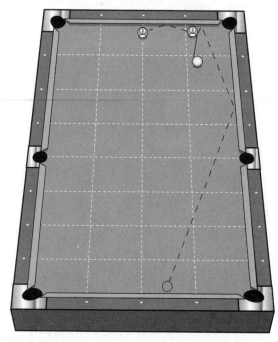

Figure 11.15 The most common response to this shot would be the well-executed safety.

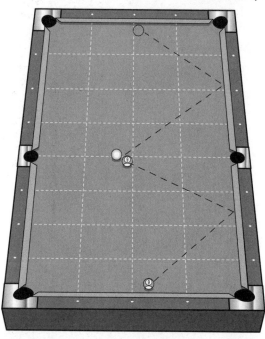

Figure 11.16 Opt for the safety with this half-ball hit scenario when no pocket exists for an offensive shot.

Much like long-distance defensive moves, short-distance moves will also boil down to three basic options. Figure 11.15 shows the more common defensive response to the previous leave (from figure 11.14). A thin cut leaves the nine ball toward the center of the short rail and sends the cue ball back down table. Note that the shot illustrated is easier for left-handed players from this side of the table.

Figure 11.16 illustrates a possible half-ball hit situation. The balls are very close together, and there is no pocket for an offensive shot. Hit this a hair thicker than a half-ball hit with no english. Where you drive the cue ball will produce a near mirror image result on the object ball to the other end of the table. This is because the half-ball hit results in half the energy left being used to send the cue ball one direction, and the remaining energy being used to send the object ball just as far in the other direction.

Figure 11.17 illustrates a really fun full-ball shot. For this shot, the nine ball can be just off any rail, and the cue ball must be almost (but not quite) frozen to the nine. Here the cue ball and nine ball are so close together that any follow-through whatsoever runs the risk of a double hit. To avoid this problem, you must take an unconventional approach. Set your cue stick on the table behind the shot as shown. Be sure that the tip is actually under the outer edge of the ball. Grab the shaft with just your thumb and forefinger a couple of inches behind the tip. Do not hold the butt end of the cue! Then, simply lift the front end of your cue quickly so that the cue tip knocks the edge of the cue ball and ever-so-gently sends it into the object ball, which will contact the cushion for a legal hit. (Note: Lift your cue up and keep it up!) Your opponent may cry foul on this, but the rules state that as long as it's the cue tip contacting the cue ball, it's legal.

Finally, you can apply the knowledge you used in the previous example of the offensive throw shot to throwing a frozen ball shot for a safety. Check out this amazing shot in figure 11.18. True, it's not easy, but with the balls left in this position, what's a player to do? Speed is critical, as is the spin to get the cue ball back down the table.

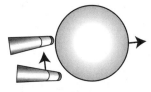

Figure 11.17 Here's a tricky shot you might want to check on the rule for in advance. Technically, it's legal but will your local tournament director know that?

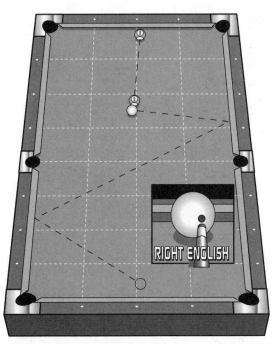

RIGHT ENGLISH

Figure 11.18 The perfect shot with which to wind up the day and your advanced lesson in 9-Ball game winners!

Practice each one of the shot situations we've illustrated and try to come up with similar versions of your own. The more strange and unusual shots you can remember, and, more importantly, have the proper offensive or defensive reaction to, the more games, matches and tournaments you will win! If a shot doesn't work for you consistently, develop a response to the situation that's better for your individual game strengths.

And always, shoot straight!

Index

About the Authors

Gerry "The Ghost" Kanov and Shari "The Shark" Stauch combine an unprecedented wealth of professional pool experience and talent to create this book. Both are staff members of *Pool & Billiard Magazine*, the top publication for the sport. They have played and worked with virtually every top professional pool player and instructor in the world.

Kanov has been playing professional and amateur pool since 1968. He has dozens of local and national top-three finishes and championships, including two national team championships as a player or coach. He is an instructional editor and technical advisor for *Pool & Billiard Magazine* and writes the "Ghost" and "Eight-Ball Ernie" columns.

Kanov was a touring professional on the Camel Pro Billiard series and a coach for several top players. He also has a screen credit: He portrayed a referee in the motion picture *The Color of Money*. Kanov lives in Gallatin, Tennessee.

Stauch has been on the Women's Pro Billiard Tour since 1980. She has been consistently ranked in the top 32 and is a former Illinois and Wisconsin state 9-ball champion. She is the owner and executive editor of *Pool & Billiard*

Magazine and has performed dozens of exhibitions for a variety of clients, such as ESPN, ESPN2, and Gordon's Gin and Vodka.

Stauch is the founding president of the Billiard Education Foundation, which conducts youth billiard national championships and provides scholarships. She serves as the treasurer on the Women's Professional Billiard Association (WPBA) board of directors and was the public relations director of the World Confederation of Billiard Sports, an international federation that succeeded in getting pool recognized was an official Olympic sport for the 2000 Games. Stauch was also involved with *The Color of Money*, serving as a consultant. She lives in Summerville, South Carolina.